ER
IC
AN
AMNESIA

How We Lost Our National Memory—and How to Recover It

HELEN E. KRIEBLE

New York • London

© 2022 by Vernon K. Krieble Foundation

All rights reserved. No part of this publication may be reproduced, stored in a retrieval system, or transmitted, in any form or by any means, electronic, mechanical, photocopying, recording, or otherwise, without the prior written permission of Encounter Books, 900 Broadway, Suite 601, New York, New York, 10003.

First American edition published in 2022 by Encounter Books, an activity of Encounter for Culture and Education, Inc., a nonprofit, tax-exempt corporation. Encounter Books website address: www.encounterbooks.com

Manufactured in the United States and printed on acid-free paper. The paper used in this publication meets the minimum requirements of ANSI/NISO Z39.48-1992 (R 1997) (*Permanence of Paper*).

FIRST AMERICAN EDITION

LIBRARY OF CONGRESS CATALOGING-IN-PUBLICATION DATA

Names: Krieble, Helen E., 1943–2021, author.
Title: American amnesia: how we lost our national memory—and how to recover it / by Helen E. Krieble.
Description: New York: Encounter Books, 2022.
Includes bibliographical references and index.
Identifiers: LCCN 2022007487 (print) | LCCN 2022007488 (ebook)
ISBN 9781641772808 (hardcover) | ISBN 9781641772815 (ebook)
Subjects: LCSH: National characteristics, American.
United States—Politics and government—Philosophy.
Founding Fathers of the United States.
Citizenship—United States. | Liberty—United States.
Conservatism—United States. | Collective memory—United States.
Classification: LCC E169.1 .K6886 2022 (print) | LCC E169.1 (ebook)
DDC 973—dc23/eng/20220328
LC record available at https://lccn.loc.gov/2022007487
LC ebook record available at https://lccn.loc.gov/2022007488

1 2 3 4 5 6 7 8 9 20 22

CONTENTS

FOREWORD

Edwin J. Feulner

Helen Krieble was a force of nature. When she saw a problem, she examined it and decided if it was worth her attention. If it was, she committed herself to doing everything within her power to solve it.

Her parents, Bob and Nancy Krieble, of Old Lyme, CT, taught Helen early that just because something had challenged the ingenuity of thoughtful people for many years, it might be within her grasp to find the solution.

Her grandfather, Dr. Vernon K. Krieble, was a professor of chemistry and chairman of the chemistry department at Trinity College, in Hartford, CT. Her father, Dr. Robert Krieble, also earned his degrees in chemistry and was a role model problem-solver.

Bob once told me how he and his father had made their major discovery: "Ed, it was a simple idea: a threaded nut and bolt could be attached and removed whenever you wanted them to be. But, what if, when the nut and bolt are attached, you want them to stay that way? Then, what if while attached, they shake and vibrate and come loose? Maybe instead of mechanically trying to tighten them further, or welding them together, or trying to find another mechanical solution, instead you tighten them and then add a drop of a bonding chemical? That was the basic idea that led my father and me to conduct hundreds of experiments—the trial-and-error method—to find the right chemical compound that would hold the nut and bolt together permanently. That was the basic idea of what became Loctite."

Bob served as a trustee of The Heritage Foundation for more than twenty years while I served as its president. He would fly himself to Heritage board meetings at our Washington headquarters. Nothing unusual about that, I thought, until he showed me a picture of his hand-built, small wooden airplane; a machine, that in my untutored manner, would have done the Wright Brothers proud! Thank goodness he had Loctite to hold his plane's parts together, I thought, as I politely declined his offer of a ride with him in it.

I recount these Krieble family stories to illustrate the stock from which Helen Krieble came. In *American Amnesia*, Helen asks, who are we? Is America really an exceptional place? Her book both sets forth those principles and answers that fundamental question. Yes, she is a traditionalist—she relies on the wisdom of the Founding Fathers and their insights into the wisdom of the people.

She reminds us, as President James Madison wrote, "If Men were angels, no government would be necessary." Alas, we are not angels, and government is necessary. So, what is the best government we can design? Helen argues that the Founders have already examined that question and constructed the ideal form of government.

It is a government where the people rule. That is, sovereignty belongs to the people. We are not vassals of a ruling king, or of mandarin elitists operating from a Washington bureaucracy.

As she recounts in *American Amnesia*, the founding principles of America were extraordinarily strong in her native Connecticut. Therefore, Connecticut should be the showcase for America's founding principles; and if it isn't, something should be done to bring it back to that leadership role. Therefore, she asks herself, what can I do to make that happen? She decides to try some of her ideas in her home state. She creates a foundation in the name of her late grandfather, the Vernon K. Krieble Foundation, and she finds ways to recognize the wisdom of ordinary Americans who are problem-solvers. She encourages them, and she rewards them for their individual ideas to deal with real American challenges by giving out

Unsung Heroes Awards. Maybe it's encouraging civic literacy in her adopted Colorado, or recognizing the unique characteristics of individual state think tanks around the country.

When Helen Krieble saw a problem, no matter how large, she would ask: How can we solve this? Yes, this is a characteristic that she shared with many other Americans because, as she admits, "Americans have an insatiable need to fix every single problem," even though that too often involves governmental solutions. Watching from the sidelines as some of Washington's best and brightest people considered an issue, she would ask why a simple alternative way to look at the problem hadn't been proposed. Sometimes the political insiders would reply that the politicians didn't want to solve it, because the unsolved problem could be a political advantage to them. Other times, they might actually admit that the usual solution of throwing more government money at it would not really solve the problem, but would grow the governmental bureaucracies and lessen the options for real solutions available in the future. Very infrequently, these same self-proclaimed experts would admit they hadn't really thought outside the box to look for a totally new way to confront an issue. Helen would explain to them that a new way would start with going back to the Founder's first principles.

Helen would examine an issue and, often enough, find the missing link that could provide a new way of looking at a vexing policy issue. Hence, her Red Card Solution to the immigration challenge that has perplexed politicians and policy geeks for decades. In a nutshell, her solution is to use private-sector capabilities to match job opportunities with available talent, avoid the governmental bureaucratic bottlenecks, and bring the demand for specific talented labor into balance with the demand for it. Yes, there's more to it than that, as she explains in Chapter Four.

Inevitably, Helen wanted to view major policy issues through what she called the "Lens of Liberty." That identifying label became a stream of one-minute recorded spots carried on radio stations around the nation to encourage and inspire Americans to approach problems in a different way.

Helen shows us how the private sector, through a combination of rewards and incentives, can come to grips with our nation's challenges—large and small. She discusses those challenges and some of the entrepreneurial ways to solve them in this provocative volume.

The Founders established a system of government of the people, not just for meeting the people's desires, but for keeping government power in check.

Helen's plea to return to reading and understanding America's founding principles is the greatest task she has assigned to all of us. If enough sensible, real American heroes are willing to take up the challenge, then Helen's generation can be proud of the legacy they have left to the future.

Having learned from her own family, she raised her three children—Fred, Amanda, and Chris—to share her commitment to building a better America. They are the trustees of the Vernon K. Krieble Foundation.

Now, a year after their mother's passing, they carry on the family's beliefs in the validity of the Founders' principles and how they can inspire our understanding of sound government, free of political correctness, and based on a true understanding of how Americans should live, and how we can build an even freer society.

I can think of no better way to take up Helen Krieble's challenge than to read this slender volume, to remind ourselves of the principles under which we should be governed, learn from the Founders, and apply Helen's practical lessons to the local and national political issues we face.

Thanks for taking us back to basics, Helen.

Onward!

Edwin J. Feulner, PhD
Founder and president emeritus
The Heritage Foundation

June 2022

PREFACE

Helen E. Krieble (1943–2021) was raised in Connecticut, educated at the Harvard Radcliffe Institute and the University of Pennsylvania, was an assistant professor at Hartford College for Women, and a regent at the University of Hartford. She served on numerous boards and commissions, and founded and led the Vernon K. Krieble Foundation (VKK).

She was active in a bewildering array of nonprofit organizations, receiving dozens of awards for supporting free enterprise and entrepreneurship. Among them, she was a board member and patron of the renowned Leadership Program of the Rockies, and its affiliate program in her home state of Connecticut, the Charter Oak Leadership Program. But it was as an innovator of ideas on important issues that she became most highly regarded. She was covered by Fox News, CNBC, the *Wall Street Journal*, *Christian Science Monitor*, *Financial Times*, *Roll Call*, *The Hill*, *National Journal*, *American Spectator*, Human Events, *Congressional Quarterly*, and dozens of other daily papers and radio shows. Helen's speeches, writings, and radio broadcasts on the duties of American citizenship earned respect and admiration across the country. She is remembered as one of the most energetic and feisty leaders of the conservative movement, traits also common to her grandfather, father, and her own children who carry on the activist tradition.

Helen established the VKK in 1984 in honor of her grandfather, Professor Vernon K. Krieble (1885–1964), a scientist, educator, inventor, and entrepreneur. He was raised on a Pennsylvania Dutch farm, and became one of the most influential chemists in the country. He chaired the chemistry department at Trinity College for thirty-five years, and published numerous papers in the *Journal of the American Chemical Society*. Dr. Krieble perfected an anaerobic polymer that sealed metal parts to avoid vibration and leakage, and prevented nuts and bolts from loosening. Together with his son Dr. Robert Krieble (also a chemist), he founded the Loctite Corporation to market the sealant. The company is today the world's leading manufacturer of specialty sealants, with operations in eighty countries. Its products are used in everyday items from computers, automobiles, and airplanes, to vacuum cleaners and mobile phones.

Under the leadership of Robert Krieble, Helen's father, Loctite Corporation prospered and developed the first practical "Superglue." He also became a legendary leader in public-policy circles, especially for his leadership in the 1970s of the effort to educate people behind the Iron Curtain about freedom and democracy. Considered a prime mover in the struggle that eventually toppled the Soviet empire, he was also an original leader of the Heritage Foundation, the Free Congress Foundation, and several other important public-policy think tanks. He instilled in his own children, including Helen, a commitment to free-market principles, and a lifelong interest in public policy.

The Vernon K. Krieble Foundation is a relatively small public-policy organization, not a gigantic endowment, and it has limited resources. It was founded by one person—Helen Krieble—and has never had a full-time staff. Yet, with a clearly defined purpose to preserve America's founding principles, its work has called attention to the important duties of American citizenship and related issues for nearly four decades. The VKK has refocused the debate on several important issues, and persuaded leaders to a new way of thinking about America. Helen continually reminded people that the foundation's assets were the product of a free and democratic society, and of the free-enterprise system, not government. She considered it a sacred duty to use those assets "to further democratic capitalism and to preserve and promote a society of free, educated, healthy, and creative individuals." The Krieble family's work stands as proof that a handful of committed citizens can make a tremendous difference.

Helen and her three children, Amanda, Fred, and Chris, served as the VKK board, becoming involved in a variety of national issues, from strategic missile defense and illegal immigration, to the responsibilities of American citizenship. The VKK proposal for a private-sector initiative to break the difficult political deadlock on illegal immigration, known as the "Red Card Solution," attracted major press attention and helped inform the national debate about solutions through two administrations and several congressional reform attempts. The proposal was embraced by many national and state leaders as a workable solution based on a principle as old as America itself—the free market.

Helen's "Lens of Liberty" project was developed to educate Americans on what it means to be a citizen of the United States, and on the responsibilities that come with citizenship. The VKK has also supported dozens of nonprofit charitable and educational organizations that demonstrate leadership in furthering those objectives, "so that future generations can aspire to and achieve their full potential in a free society."

For several years Helen recorded a series of radio minutes, aired on more than 800 radio stations, reminding Americans to look at all issues through the "lens of liberty." She gave the "Unsung Hero Award" at annual meetings of the State Policy Network, a $25,000 prize recognizing everyday people who fought for freedom in their communities, and similar student hero awards at Turning Point USA meetings, including a $10,000 prize for college students who stood up for liberty on campuses. She also produced two documentary films, one on the Red Card Solution and another promoting a broader understanding of citizenship. Her frequent op-ed pieces helped draw attention to the relationship between founding principles and contemporary issues.

Another VKK initiative was the "American Citizenship Owner's Manual," which explained America's founding ideals and its unique system of self-government. Thousands of copies were distributed at the Conservation Political Action Conference (CPAC) and other gatherings popular with young voters. Other publications included a modern-language translation of America's founding documents, making them more accessible to young readers, and several thousand "Freedom Kits" were created to be used by volunteers and activists across the country. VKK also helped the Bill of Rights Institute develop new curriculum materials focused on the responsibilities of American citizenship.

Helen was a frequent speaker, and she and her family were regular fixtures for many years at events for CPAC, State Policy Network, the Heritage Foundation, Americans for Tax Reform, Free Congress Foundation, and FreedomFest, as well as at college campuses and numerous other conferences and meetings. Today, under the leadership of Fred Krieble, the VKK continues its important work for America's founding principles, and the Krieble family continues its long tradition of philanthropy and public service.

INTRODUCTION

Our memories quite literally make us who we are.

Memories create character. That process begins with our earliest childhood memories, and continues through the lessons of the classroom and far beyond. Our lives are made up of experiences with families, friends, businesses, and communities. In turn, those experiences mold our personalities, our quirks, our sense of humor, our foibles, our strengths and weaknesses. We learn from experiences our sense of right and wrong, our personal priorities, our work ethic, and even our political views.

Like most people, I sometimes forget where I laid something down, why I came into a room, or even where I parked the car. I empathize with the late Betty White, who once said she got lots of exercise because she had a two-story house and a bad memory.

Some say memory is a fleeting thing, like fame or glory. But it's much more than that, because we are never content with the idea that memories come and go. We want to hold onto the things we know. We don't want to study everything we need to know, each time we need to know it. We don't have time to relearn everything that has accumulated in our brain. But memory is far more than merely recollecting information as needed.

The novelist Grant Allen famously wrote, "I have never let my schooling interfere with my education." (The quote is often attributed incorrectly to Mark Twain.) That is a clever way of explaining that knowledge comes from experiences as much as from schools, and that education never stops, but continues throughout life. As we grow older, we grow wiser, and our perspective broadens because of the accumulation of memories.

Whether or not we are blessed with exceptionally good memories, though, we are who we are because of what we have been through, where we have come from, who we have learned from, and all the things that have happened to us.

The same is true not just for individuals, but also for families, communities, and nations. Our country, too, has its own unique character, also formed by its memories, its history, all the things it has been through, and what it has learned.

We know that when individuals lose their memory, they lose their character. The tragedy of Alzheimer's, and dementia in all its forms, devastates millions of families as loved ones slowly fade away, unable to remember people, places, and events. They are still present physically, but clearly not the same people they once were. Their character is altered and utterly diminished.

What if a nation loses its memory? Its character is also altered and diminished. That is why people of various cultures throughout the world work so hard to maintain their identity, and to pass traditions along to future generations. In many Native American societies, each family chooses one person to continue the storytelling tradition, and to pass along languages, songs, customs, and tribal history. Oral traditions play an important part in community life. Similarly, in many West African tribes, a griot is so respected as the historian, storyteller, and genealogist that he becomes a key leader and an advisor to kings. This reflects the widespread understanding that good decisions require an understanding of history, in governments of all sizes and types.

When European explorers first encountered natives of the South Pacific islands during the seventeenth century, they were shocked by the varying levels of civilization on different islands. As science writer Matt Ridley explains, those islands were settled thousands of years ago by people originally from the same parts of the world, arriving in very similar canoes. But in the absence of written language, those early civilizations relied heavily on one generation passing knowledge along to the next. Some did, and some did not.

The result was that over time, some islands lost the knowledge of boat-building and sailing, while other islands continued trade and commerce, evolving to a much higher level of civilization by the time of European contact. That is why the European explorers found more advanced cultures in Samoa and Tahiti, and extremely primitive ones in Tasmania and Vanuatu.

Ridley argues that larger civilizations are more apt to pass along acquired knowledge, and smaller ones more likely to lose it, if for no other reason than larger civilizations have more people to worry about it, and more resources to spend on it. But what if a nation purposely decides it no longer wants to remember its history? What if a country imposes amnesia on itself? Could a civilization as large and advanced as the United States, the world's most industrialized and modern superpower, lose its own understanding of the lessons learned from its own history?

Today's educational journals are filled with reports on how poorly American students perform when tested on history, civics, government, and other social studies. Three-quarters of graduating seniors cannot demonstrate a proficient understanding of America's founding principles, its constitutional system, the history of its institutions, or its governmental procedures. That does not mean the current generation of students is less intelligent than previous generations, as shown by their continued impressive achievements in other fields. Rather, it is the result of an educational system that has simply stopped teaching much of our history and civics.

That doesn't matter just because we want our children to pass tests and get good grades. Nor is it just about wanting everybody to do their civic duty and vote in local, state, and national elections. It matters because in the United States' sovereignty belongs to the people, not the government. "We the people" are the owners—the managing partners. We cannot manage responsibly what we do not understand, any more than someone could run a hamburger stand without knowing how to make a hamburger.

Americans' understanding of their own history and government has been declining for years, as these subjects have become less important to the education establishment. But our citizens have acquiesced in that decline, and attach far less importance to history than previous generations did. In fact, much of today's popular culture includes themes showing only the dark side of American culture and history, often portrayed as imperialistic, racist, and unfair. We now teach that America is just one of many cultures in the world, no better than any other, worse than some, and we are all citizens of the world. Such themes permeate the news media, Hollywood, the music industry, schools, and the Internet.

No wonder, after years of such messages, Americans are losing their appreciation for their unique system of government. Pollsters attest that fewer than half of Americans today believe their government system is better than others around the world. No wonder a 2012 presidential candidate's use of the phrase "American exceptionalism" became a hotly debated point. Vast numbers of Americans no longer see their country as exceptional. Our self-imposed amnesia is taking hold.

America was founded as a great experiment in self-government, a laughing stock of all the monarchies and noble houses of Europe, who believed the new nation would inevitably fail because common people could never govern themselves. Abraham Lincoln understood the Civil War was not just about slavery or states' rights, but about whether any government "so conceived and so dedicated can long endure." We still struggle in a world of people who think democracy is doomed to failure.

America's founding generation understood a fundamental truth: a democratic republic can only work if the people understand it. America only works if its people understand its history and the important ideals upon which it is built. They must know that *e pluribus unum*, our national motto, means our strength comes not from diversity, but from unity; from our commitment to a form of government based on the responsible individual and the right to life, liberty, and the pursuit of happiness. This is what makes our democracy unique in the world and our people one.

As we lose our national memory of these principles, and the sacrifices made over the past 250 years to preserve them, we are losing our national character. America cannot be preserved as "the last best hope of Earth" (as Lincoln memorably described the United States) if our own people no longer understand why that is true and are no longer willing to do what it takes to preserve it. The duties of citizenship are vitally important, but they are not complicated. It is our duty, as the owners, to defend our freedom against all threats, and to pass it along to future generations undiminished.

We are failing in that duty, but there is still time to cure our national amnesia. Hundreds of thousands of activists across the country are enlisting in the effort to rebuild our commitment to founding principles, to regain our memory, and recapture our exceptionalism. Our great national experiment in democracy must not be lost by our generation—not on our watch.

CHAPTER ONE

WHO ARE WE?

R osa Parks was one of America's indispensable civil rights icons, Rita Hayworth one of its great actresses, Ronald Reagan one of its most consequential presidents, and Norman Rockwell one of its most beloved artists. They all had something else in common, along with 700,000 Americans who die with Alzheimer's disease every year. All four of them suffered memory losses so thorough and tragic that they eventually had no knowledge of who they were, how important they had been, and why their lives had mattered to millions.

These and many other sufferers were fortunate enough to have family members and other caregivers to help when they lost their character. Will the United States be as fortunate? American society is losing its character because of its acute memory loss, too, with millions of citizens no longer aware of America's history, and what it has meant to generations of people around the world. This nation needs more than caregivers to supply day-to-day needs, though. Americans need to be reminded of who they are, and why their character matters.

What exactly is America's national "character"? There are almost as many descriptions as there are Americans, and today's opinion leaders disagree on what it means to be an American. Politicians routinely criticize each other with the easy throw-away line, "That's just not who we are." The very fact that there is a national debate about it underscores the problem: Americans as a whole do not understand what is so special about their unique place in the world, and in the history of freedom. So, who are we?

From the very first European settlements in America, both at Plymouth and at Jamestown, colonists almost immediately developed a different character than their ancestors in the old world. A rugged individualism began to develop very early, largely because of the circumstances of the land itself—a new world where everyone had to work if they wanted to eat. The land itself served to unite rich and poor alike under the banner of equality. Among the first settlers at Jamestown, and on the Mayflower a few years later, there were people of wealth and upbringing, often from some of the most prominent families in Europe. They sailed on the same boats with farmers, merchants, tradesmen, and people so poor they sold themselves into indentured servitude in order to pay their passage to America—people with whom the noble families would never have mingled back home. Yet even many of the wealthy settlers faced the same oppressive lack of opportunity in Europe as the poor, because they were not the firstborn sons.

Primogeniture, the system under which lands, positions, and titles were inherited by the firstborn sons, had been in place in Europe for centuries, and it left generations of people with at least modest wealth and first-class educations, but no prospects for a better future. They often had as much reason to come to a new land of opportunity as their poor shipmates. Many of the early settlers were the second or third sons of English aristocracy; others were aristocrats' daughters, some of whom were granted land in the new colonies—something they could never have achieved in England. In fact, King James II was said to have derisively referred to America as "the second sons' colonies," a nickname that stuck for many years.

In the South, those wealthier settlers became the planter class, and in New England the merchant class. In Pennsylvania, William Penn dreamed of turning his own land grant into a colony for "common people," providing opportunity for the poor to prosper alongside the second sons of England. At Jamestown, Captain John Smith had turned the reality of "everyone works if they want to eat" into law. While the colonies in different regions evolved differently, they all shared that common theme of equality.

Equality as a principle may have developed as the culture of the American colonies out of necessity at first, since it certainly did not come naturally to Europeans. But it nonetheless became deeply embedded in the psyche of the colonists. By the time of the American Revolution, the idea that all are equal in the eyes of the law had been part of the American culture for generations. Moreover, the concept that ordinary people could govern themselves was far more than an abstract notion of philosophers. By that time, it was the proven experience of Americans, whose isolation from the "civilized world" of Europe left no choice but to govern themselves. That made them unique among the world's varied cultures, and has made their exceptional system the envy of millions ever since.

At the beginning of Barack Obama's presidency, he touched off a firestorm of criticism about "American exceptionalism" and what it meant. He, and others, questioned if it even existed. By the end of his tenure, supporters were openly praising him for "redefining" the concept. The *Washington Post* called him "a tinkerer and a poet in whose hands the concept of 'American exceptionalism' is being reshaped for the twenty-first century and weaponized against Trumpism." That misunderstanding is not only sad, it is dangerous for the future of America. It is now being transmitted to younger Americans through our schools, churches, TV programming, and social media outlets.

We now have a president in Joe Biden who has echoed the cries of those on the extreme left, who say that America is "systemically racist."

The notion that there is an Obama version, or a Trump version, or a Biden version of American exceptionalism belittles and misses the truth: that there are principles and characteristics of America far greater than Obama, Trump, Biden, or any other leader.

AMERICAN EXCEPTIONALISM

The concept of American exceptionalism was first identified, and discussed at length, by Alexis de Tocqueville in the 1830s, when he published two large volumes attempting to explain the uniqueness of America to his fellow Frenchmen. Unlike European societies dominated by aristocrats, he characterized the United States as a society where hard work and personal improvement were the central theme, and where the common man enjoyed an equal level of dignity. In his observation, it was unprecedented that commoners never "deferred" to elites, as was expected in Europe, and he described a crass individualism and free-market ethic that had taken root among Americans.

Tocqueville's description of the American work ethic defined the "American dream," as it is often called now. "Among a democratic people, where there is no hereditary wealth, every man works to earn a living," he wrote. "Labor is held in honor." In old European societies, laborers were looked down upon, so the contrast was palpable. That led to his observation that a rapidly democratizing society had a citizenry devoted to achieving fortunes through hard work. It explained a crucial difference between the US and Europe, where Tocqueville said nobody cared about making money. The lower classes had no hope of gaining wealth, and the upper classes thought it vulgar to discuss their birthright. Yet by contrast, far from being envious or jealous, Tocqueville said that when American workers saw people fashionably dressed and well-heeled, they simply announced that through hard work they would soon have such things, too.

Americans have come a long way from that rich history. Today, they are frequently told that their strength as a society lies in ethnic diversity, not in unity of purpose. The uniqueness of America is more often misunderstood than well-articulated. It is often expressed as a superficial superiority, that the US is the richest and most powerful country on Earth.

In his now-famous 2009 press conference, Obama was asked to explain his "enthusiasm for multilateral frameworks," and his view of American exceptionalism. He replied, "I believe in American exceptionalism, just as I suspect that the Brits believe in British exceptionalism and the Greeks believe in Greek exceptionalism." He further explained,

> Now, the fact that I am very proud of my country and I think that we've got a whole lot to offer the world does not lessen my interest in recognizing the value and wonderful qualities of other countries, or recognizing that we're not always going to be right, or that other people may have good ideas, or that in order for us to work collectively, all parties have to compromise, and that includes us.

For the rest of his tenure in office, he never escaped the accusation by some that he didn't love America enough. He made a point of using the word "exceptional" afterwards, but many critics just didn't believe him. Perhaps that was because he had such difficulty articulating precisely what was so exceptional, or special, about America. He often spoke about America's role in defending and rebuilding Europe during and after World War II as a source of great pride. He mentioned the US having the world's largest economy and an unmatched military capability. He told the Business Roundtable in 2014,

> When you ask people now, what is the number one place to invest, it's the United States of America. [...] A lot of that has to do with the fact that we've got the best workers in the world, we've got the best university system, and research and development and innovation in the world, and we've got the best businesses in the world.

He told the National Institutes of Health that same month that, "Part of American leadership in the world—one of the things that has always marked us as exceptional—is our leadership in science and our leadership in research." In a speech praising health care workers who went to West Africa to combat Ebola, he said,

> A lot of people talk about American exceptionalism. I'm a firm believer in American exceptionalism. You know why I am? It's because of folks like this. It's because we don't run and hide when there's a problem. […] It is people who are willing to go there at significant sacrifice to make a difference. That's American exceptionalism. That's what we should be proud of. That's who we are.

Americans can take pride in having the world's strongest economy, unmatched military, best workers, top universities, and leadership in research, development, and health care, among many others. They can also be proud of the generosity of Americans who travel the world helping those less fortunate. They are a brave, independent, entrepreneurial, virtuous, and generous people. But other cultures can also be charitable; there are several other very strong economies, and numerous military powerhouses. Many other nations also invest heavily in health care, education, and technological research. These are important, but they are *not* what makes America unique. They are a result of national exceptionalism, not the source of it.

For years Americans have been bombarded by political and cultural leaders lecturing about the importance of diversity. President Clinton said, "My fellow Americans, we must never believe that our diversity is a weakness. It is our greatest strength." President Obama went further, "The world respects us not just for our arsenal; it respects us for our diversity." Strength from diversity has been a common theme of the last fifty years, readily found in speeches by leaders of the UN, the USSR, India, New York City, London, France, Uganda, and many others. "Diversity, our strength" is the official motto of Toronto, Canada, but not of the United States of America. In fact, it is diametrically opposite to the American motto *e pluribus unum* which stresses unity, not diversity. Yet the joke nowadays, that is too close to the truth, is that many of our citizens believe the American motto of *e pluribus unum* means "out of one, many."

All of this preoccupation with race as a dividing line in America may seem ironic, given that the United States has a more diverse population than any other nation. There is no question that diversity adds to the society's rich character, as well as contributes to many of its traditions. But America's strength, and especially its endurance, do not spring from its diversity. They come from its unity.

Americans of all backgrounds are united behind a set of governing principles. That is the source of American exceptionalism. It is a unity that transcends party politics, race, color, religion, national origin, gender, or any other human trait. In America, it does not matter where your family came from, what language your parents spoke, or who you are related to.

Americans are united by a belief in the essential principle that ordinary people can govern themselves, and that the primary role of government is to protect their right to do so.

That principle is what defines Americans. In fact, among such a vastly diverse population that includes elements of every other culture in the world, it is the *only* truly unifying theme. That is what has held this diverse country together for nearly 250 years.

HOW THE MIGHTY HAVE FALLEN

The same Alexis de Tocqueville, whose seminal work on American democracy in the 1830s extolled the virtues of a free society, also foresaw some of its greatest challenges. In fact, his warnings were mostly ignored, and have largely come true.

He warned especially about the omnipotence and all-powerful character of the majority in a democratic system. He knew that unchecked political power inevitably leads to tyranny, and warned that such power is just as dangerous in the hands of an unchecked majority of citizens as in the hands of a king or dictator. Thus, the greatest danger Americans faced, what he called the "tyranny of the majority," could already be seen in their mistreatment of minorities.

The Bill of Rights was adopted specifically to guard Americans' individual rights, especially against abuses of power, but they were mainly worded as restrictions against the government, not the people themselves. For instance, the First Amendment guaranteed that "Congress shall make no law [...] abridging the freedom of speech" but that does not guard against angry mobs shouting down speakers on college campuses. In fact, one of Tocqueville's most shocking claims, from today's perspective, is that there was less freedom of discussion and "independence of mind" in America than in Europe, such was the power of peer pressure, the human tendency to follow the crowd, and the fear of angry mobs. Today, many students are taught and believe that people don't have the right to say things that might "offend" others.

Several observers over the past two centuries have worried that Americans might discover the ability to vote themselves benefits from the public treasury, or to make other policy mistakes that endanger their own future as a republic. Tocqueville put it elegantly, "It is not necessary to do violence to such a people in order to strip them of the rights they enjoy; they themselves willingly loosen their hold. [...] They neglect their chief business, which is to remain their own masters."

That prediction has come true, and today Americans face an uncertain future because their national character is no longer rooted in fierce individualism and personal responsibility. Instead, they have opted for massive public benefits at the expense of future generations, completely ignoring the economic disaster that will eventually cause (not to mention the morality of leaving such debt behind). Some observers now think that unfathomable public debt is the only thing that still unites a politically and socially divided people.

Perhaps worse, citizens have demanded, and Congress has delivered, ever increasing levels of government regulation over virtually every aspect of modern life—almost none of which was envisioned by the Constitution. Today's mass of government agencies, laws, rules, permits, and enforcement is the furthest thing imaginable from citizens "remaining their own masters."

America's founders envisioned a system of "checks and balances," to insure against a powerful government usurping or abusing the sovereign power that belongs to the people. So, they wrote the Constitution to embody a system of carefully divided responsibilities, where each branch of government has a distinct responsibility in preserving the people's rights: Congress legislates, the President administers, and the courts provide independent judgment in contested cases. But the federal system no longer works that way. Today, the executive branch not only administers, but also makes laws, and sits in judgement. The courts, now, not only sit in judgment, but also make laws, and enforce their judgments. Meanwhile, Congress has delegated most of its legislative authority to executive branch agencies. The constitutional lines separating the branches are now almost nonexistent.

A group called the New Civil Liberties Alliance has tracked and reported on the massive growth of "administrative law," that is, rules and regulations enacted by executive branch agencies, not by Congress, and enforced by executive branch agencies, not by courts. Its conclusions are frightening. "Americans accused of violations are now ten times more likely to be tried by an unelected bureaucrat than by a federal judge." For example, the IRS, has evolved into a tax collection agency that operates on the principle that you are guilty until you can prove yourself innocent.

Pointing out that Congress now enacts fewer than 100 laws per year (many of them on superficial subjects such as naming buildings), the group points out that Congress is "handing over the task of legislating to federal administrative agencies. This Administrative State now enforces and adjudicates hundreds of thousands of regulations governing daily activities in our lives."

Keeping in mind the founding declaration that government only "derives its just powers from the consent of the governed," this administrative usurpation could only happen with the consent of the people themselves. It is by inaction that Americans have *consented* to the steady chipping away of their principles, and their freedom.

My home state of Connecticut is in many ways a microcosm of the growth of government, the loss of personal freedoms, and the devastating impact on the state's economy, culture, and way of life.

THE CHARTER OAK

The "Charter Oak" may be Connecticut's most famous icon, a symbol of liberty, independence, and self-reliance for more than 300 years. A picture of the tree was used on a commemorative half-dollar in the 1930s, and on Connecticut's state quarter in the 1990s. The image is now a logo for dozens of organizations and the name Charter Oak is on a bank, several parks, a state college, a bridge, a hospital, several restaurants, a vinyl siding company, stereo equipment, machine shop manufacturers, and even a brewery. References to the charter oak are so common that few people even wonder about its origin or think about its symbolism. It is worth remembering.

Connecticut's original charter, the document providing for self-government of a free people, was granted by King James I in 1622, but sixty-five years later King James II tried to take it back. Other colonies had voluntarily surrendered their charters, but not Connecticut. So, the King sent an officer and soldiers to seize control and confiscate the charter. On an October evening in 1687, with the charter on the table between the parties, the officer demanded surrender, and tempers flared. Suddenly the candles were extinguished and in the darkness the charter disappeared. Capt. Joseph Wadsworth had grabbed the paper and hidden it in the hollow of the old tree out back. The soldiers took over by force, but only temporarily. James II was overthrown just a year later, and the preserved charter resurfaced. It remained the governing document of the colony, thanks to the bravery of a few citizens who refused to surrender their freedom.

That famous white oak tree was said to be 1,000 years old, and had a hollow trunk in which twenty-seven men could stand, so it was the perfect hiding place. It thus became a venerated place in Hartford, standing near what is now the corner of Charter Oak

Avenue and Charter Oak Place. The original tree is gone, perhaps a fitting emblem of the decline of freedom and prosperity in a state that once created America's first written Constitution.

Today, Connecticut is in dire straits, failing financially, and failing its citizens, too. Once an international center for industry and commerce, Connecticut is now losing its population. Between 2018-2021, more than 75,000 residents left, taking with them more than $2.6 billion in income. The state used to be called the "The Insurance Capital of the World," but most of the largest insurance companies have departed for a better economic, regulatory, and tax environment elsewhere. Greenwich was considered the "Hedge Fund Capital," but billions in funds and their principals have moved to other states, along with historic manufacturing, tool-and-die, and other important employers. In 2016, General Electric relocated its headquarters from Fairfield to Boston. Pharmaceutical companies are leaving. Defense companies are leaving. The state's wealthiest citizens, greatest revenue generators, and largest job creators are all leaving.

The capital city of Hartford is on the verge of bankruptcy and its unfunded pension obligations cannot be met. The University of Connecticut is losing critical funding, and education at every level is in decline. Budget deficits are expected to be $2 billion a year for the next several years.

How is this possible in the nation's wealthiest state? How has it gone from a bastion of freedom, growth, and affluence, to a state whose citizens and businesses suffer under some of the country's highest taxes and most burdensome regulations? This noble state's affairs have been mismanaged for years, and the freedom of its people has been slowly chipped away.

Year after year, Connecticut politicians fail to represent the best interests of the state, and yet its citizens continue to hope that the next set of politicians will reverse the downward spiral. But they have not done so. For more than thirty years, governors and legislators of both parties have continued to grow government, raise taxes, and pile on more regulations. They have forgotten the famous admonition that insanity is doing the same thing over and over again, and expecting a different outcome.

It is past time for citizens to hold Connecticut's leaders accountable. They must remind officials that freedom is not a thing of the past, but an expectation for both the present and the future. A state that was the original cradle of American democracy is barely a shell of its once-fierce independent self, like the hollowed-out trunk of a dying tree—but without the old oak's stately pride.

The ancient tree finally collapsed during a violent storm in 1857, but its story does not end there. Its acorns had been collected for years, and were used to plant dozens of descendants. Those clones can be seen in Hartford's Bushnell Park, at the post office in Collinsville, the Union Society in Eastford, Pine Street in Middletown, and the Florence Griswold Museum in Old Lyme. Thus, the tree never completely died, nor should its symbolism. The people of Connecticut nurture offspring from the Charter Oak all across the state. They must also relearn to nurture the freedom it once stood for.

THE STEADY EROSION OF FREEDOM

The individual rights guaranteed to all Americans have been chipped away, little by little, without anyone ever having decided on such a plan. It has happened slowly and incrementally, but in response to demands by the citizens themselves. That's because Americans have an insatiable need to fix every single problem, or at least try to do so. Unfortunately, they have been told that almost always requires government action, regardless of the obvious reality that many problems in life cannot be solved by government.

It is a virtual cliché that when Americans sense something is wrong, they respond with: "There ought to be a law." The result is an unseemly and un-American expectation of government programs that care for us from cradle to grave. That has led to a "nanny state" view that government should decide everything and pay for everything, and an intrusiveness on the part of citizens, who no longer think of anything as "none of your business." There is virtually nothing left which is universally considered none of the government's business.

WHAT HAVE WE BECOME?

Modern liberals like to call themselves "progressives." The word implies progress, but it is a difficult concept to justify when they call for restrictions on free speech and other essential rights while building up a government that surpasses any other in history in terms of its size, power, and cost. Such views actually harken back to earlier times, not a better future. Thus, liberals should more accurately be called "regressives."

Sadly, few seem to know the difference, at least partly because these concepts were never taught in their schools. Several states have passed laws requiring graduating high school students to pass the same citizenship test required of new, naturalized immigrants. Yet numerous studies show that most Americans today could not pass that test, even though it has been simplified several times.

King George III would be so proud. He and his aristocratic friends were amused by America's quaint "experiment" with self-government. To them, it was unthinkable that common people were enlightened enough to rule themselves. That experiment is now the hope and dream of people throughout the world, but what about here in the US?

Hillsdale College's Matthew Spalding wrote a persuasive and best-selling book called *We Still Hold These Truths*. He made the case that despite shockingly poor educational outcomes, at heart, Americans still believed in the founding principles. Indeed, most people still tell pollsters they strongly believe in freedom, limited government, and personal responsibility. But do they?

Astonishingly, many Americans expect government to care for their every need, the way commoners once expected a benevolent king to care for his subjects. They treat people as members of groups rather than as individuals, which insidiously devolves into a "class" system that was the very concept against which the founders rebelled.

Today's "classes" are not based on relative wealth like those of the eighteenth century, but modern law nevertheless singles out "protected classes" based on qualities like race, color, gender, religion, national origin, sexual preference, age, disabilities, and military service. The result is unequal treatment under the law, entirely contrary to the principles of natural law expressed by the Declaration of Independence. Americans are voluntarily surrendering the very freedoms that millions have fought and died to establish and protect.

Many of the "long train of abuses" that led to America's rebellion from the British Crown are eerily similar to the excesses of America's own government today. The Declaration of Independence listed grievances against King George III that are all too familiar. The authors accused him of refusing "his assent to laws [...] necessary for the public good," of forbidding locals to pass laws "of immediate and pressing importance," even of dissolving local representative bodies.

How different is that from a Congress that cannot pass the most essential bills for annual appropriations and budgets? How different is it from today's "supreme" federal system that routinely overrides local and state laws, especially by federal court orders and "constitutional" rulings based on premises that are not in the Constitution?

The Crown had "obstructed the administration of justice" by controlling judges' tenure and salaries. Today's government does so by empowering judges to usurp legislative powers by making up new laws rather than interpreting laws passed by the people's representatives. It is a more modern technique, but with the same anti-democratic result.

King George III had "erected a multitude of new offices, and sent hither swarms of officers to harass our people and eat out their substance." By 2020, the federal government had more than four million employees, at a cost approaching $5 trillion a year. The King "combined with others to subject us to a jurisdiction foreign to our constitution," much as our modern leaders compromise America's sovereignty to institutions like the UN, international courts, the World Health Organization, and foreign trade commissions.

The founders said government should protect private property, but today's Supreme Court lets government take private property and sell it to developers, destroy the value of land by denying the right to use it, and force landowners to give up their land for endangered species habitat, parks, trails, and "open space." The first "inalienable right" in the Declaration was the right to life, but today's courts prohibit states from protecting it. If Americans still believe "all men are created equal," how can they justify racial preferences in school admission, government contracts, or congressional reapportionment? Freedom of speech is central to the Bill of Rights, but it is under attack by politically correct thought police all across America, especially at government-financed educational institutions.

"The policy of the federal government," wrote President Jefferson, "is to leave her citizens free, neither aiding nor restraining them in their pursuits." Today, Americans face restrictions on how to plan their own retirement, design their own health insurance, or even devise their own children's education. The endless intrusion reaches into every facet of their lives, from where they can hike in the woods to how their hamburgers must be cooked. Both parties instinctively look to government as the first answer to all problems. Even many Republicans propose solving issues like illegal immigration by hiring thousands more federal employees.

There is one crucial difference: unlike their colonial ancestors, contemporary Americans voluntarily agreed to all these usurpations with their votes. Voters have been warned frequently to be alert to threats against their freedom, but have often shirked that most essential duty of citizenship.

Americans have two clear choices. Do they really want to declare the America of their founders dead, and accept the mediocre socialism it has devolved into? Or, will they withdraw the "consent of the governed" and revive the American experiment that made them the freest people on earth and the envy of the world?

OUR NEW NATIONAL CHARACTER?

Today, millions of Americans watch from the sidelines as uninvolved spectators, while government leaders routinely ignore the most basic principles. The federal government has nationalized private industries from health care, child care, and electric power, to passenger rail service and airport security. Federally owned businesses compete against private enterprise in telecommunications, utilities, transportation, insurance, consumer loans, and dozens of other areas. Government dictates the terms of business in agriculture, mining, manufacturing, fishing, pharmaceuticals, broadcasting, education, and nearly every other industry. The *New York Times* recently published a front-page story with the headline that Joe Biden's budget plan would provide "cradle-to-grave government" assistance to Americans.

Leaders engage in fierce debates almost every year about the simplest of Constitutional rights, such as the Second Amendment right to keep and bear arms, and increasingly, the First Amendment right to free speech and assembly. Political correctness is effectively silencing all speech with which academic dictators disagree, on college campuses, radio and television, and in everyday workplaces. People accused of various offenses are automatically deemed guilty until proven otherwise, their careers and reputations destroyed without due process of law.

America's national identity is in danger of being erased. Many millions of Americans, like me, fear that our nation is being replaced by a borderless socialist regime that has lost its moral compass. A free people would never tolerate such abuses if they remembered their principles; if they retained the character that comes from their history. When America stops teaching that history, it risks losing that character, the rugged individualism that makes America special, unique, different, and exceptional.

The first attempts by government to expand its power were not "nipped in the bud," and today's dire situation crept up very slowly. It is the nature of all governments to expand and increase their power incrementally, so this was natural, and no doubt began as soon as the ink was dry on the Constitution. That is why its authors said only a vigilant public could prevent that, and why they thought educating the people was so important. It is why they called it the first duty of citizenship to pass along these principles to future generations. This is why we have public education in America, and yet the government schools are failing that scared mission.

But there is a problem here. This tradition of passing down the principles of American greatness has become dislodged.

People cannot pass along memories they don't have, nor can a nation. The failure to educate future generations guarantees a loss of national memory and, thus, national character. Sadly, this is happening—on purpose—as people increasingly look to government for solutions to every problem, and decline to teach history, values, principles, and civics to their children. Is the entire American system of self-government slowly and painfully committing suicide?

Angry protests and demonstrations are more common than ever in America's cities, but they lack the unifying theme that characterized such protests in the 1960s. In that era, protesters articulated a deep fear and anger about the Vietnam War, and about civil rights abuses. More recently, from Occupy Wall Street in 2011 to the 2017 Women's March, the 2020 takeover of neighborhoods in Seattle and Minneapolis, and countless others, demonstrators have had difficulty explaining exactly what they were marching for. All seemed angry, but with dozens of different causes, and with many protestors remarkably unable to tell interviewers why they were there. Some complained about "unfair" wages, others about "unequal" treatment, still others about the presence of police (who were there to protect the demonstrators' safety), and most recently, nearly every incident involving police shootings. Today, demonstrators take to the streets to protest against political views with which they disagree, seeking to shout down their adversaries, tear down statues regardless of their symbolism, and vandalize the private property of innocent people.

Numerous participants in demonstrations and riots have confirmed that they were paid to be there, but rarely does anyone seem to know where the money came from, or what the organizers hoped to accomplish. That does not mean there are no problems worthy of such activism. Rather, it is a symptom of the void left by an insufficient education in civics. Vast numbers of people simply do not understand how their government works, what it is (and is not) in charge of, and what avenues they have for redress of grievances. They have little idea of the power of engaged citizens. That lack of understanding is easily replaced with emotion, as the all-too-regular newscasts show.

On March 7, 2015, on the fiftieth anniversary of Martin Luther King's Selma-to-Montgomery march, President Obama finally expressed how the civil rights movement actually fulfilled the founder's dream. "What Selma does better than perhaps any other moment in our history is to vindicate the faith of our founders; to vindicate the idea that ordinary folks—not of high station, not born to wealth or privilege or certain religious belief—are able to shape the destiny of their nation," Obama said. "This is the most American of ideas." He was right.

That lofty rhetoric is exactly on point, yet Americans sometimes seem convinced that their history is more about slavery and other evils than it is about Dr. King and other triumphs. It is a society that loves self-criticism, to a fault. Slavery did not make America unique. Every society had slavery for thousands of years, and many still do. There is no need to sugarcoat the areas where Americans have fallen short of their own ideals. History happened and it cannot be altered.

What makes America unique in the world is not these failures (those are not unique at all), but the fact that they were overcome, and that Americans never give up, but continuously strive.

American history is a spellbinding tale of how ordinary people from all their diverse backgrounds have worked and fought together to throw off the chains of the past, and to forge a better and freer future. It is about how they continually come together, as the Constitution says, "to form a more perfect union." But that spirit, which made America a beacon of freedom and prosperity, is in sharp decline. And that puts America's future in jeopardy.

CHAPTER TWO

~~~

THE THINGS WE BELIEVE IN

In Ronald Reagan's farewell address, he famously quoted a constituent's letter saying, "You can go to live in France, but you cannot become a Frenchman. You can go to live in Germany or Turkey or Japan, but you cannot become a German, a Turk, or a Japanese. But anyone, from any corner of the Earth, can come to live in America and become an American." Only here is that true.

In fact, it has been said that anyone, anywhere, who believes in the principles of freedom and self-government is already an American at heart. That is why the United States has historically been compared to a giant "melting pot," blending people and cultures from all over the world with a remarkable assimilation that unites an incredibly diverse population. In fact, America is by far the world's most diverse nation, precisely because there is no one American race, religion, or ethnicity. Yet there is something missing from this quaint view of America.

It assumes that most everyone who comes to America automatically become an American. That assumes all US residents inherently share a common set of ideals, but it is not automatic. It requires that those ideals be taught and learned, which we know is not always the case.

The liberal Harvard sociologist Robert Putnam, author of *Bowling Alone: The Collapse and Revival of American Community,* has spent decades studying the effect of diversity on the American culture. He has begun to question whether increased diversity may in fact "corrode civil society by eroding shared values, customs, and institutions." It is a controversial view, because for at least a generation Americans have been indoctrinated to believe that diversity is the country's greatest strength. Yet it isn't the first-generation immigrants, with black or brown skin, who are peddling anti-American sentiments and elevating race as the predominant force in America. It is the third- and fourth-generation elites.

Think about the contradiction for those who believe that race and diversity are paramount in America. They are wrong. If being an American *is not* about religion, race, or ethnicity, then more religious, racial, and ethnic diversity does not strengthen what America *is* about: shared values, customs, and institutions. In other words, racial and ethnic diversity is completely independent of shared values. So, if one believes that America is not just a country, but an idea, then the mere geographic presence of people in the US does not make them Americans.

Putnam explains, "Anyone of any race or national origin can be an American, but it requires effort and desire from both the individual and the larger society." Membership in any organization requires two things. It must be offered, under whatever conditions the group imposes, and it must be accepted, with an understanding of the responsibilities it entails. That is true of Rotary Clubs, sororities, unions, trade associations, professional societies, and social clubs. It is also true of countries. In America, the conditions imposed by the society in offering citizenship to newcomers requires subscribing to its core principles and understanding the form of government that protects them.

That is what unites America's diverse population. That is why the United States is not merely a collection of Irish, Korean, English, German, French, African, Chinese, Asian, Russian, Arab, Persian, Italian, Mexican, Polynesian, Polish, Serbian, Vietnamese, and Salvadoran people (to name but a few) sharing the same piece of land. Its people have ancestry from all those places and many more, but they are united as Americans, first and foremost, because they share a set of values and principles, and they are loyal to institutions designed to preserve and protect them. But what if they are not loyal to those principles? What happens if they no longer know what those institutions and principles are? The great idea that is America shatters. In that case, amnesia is lethal to the nation.

WHAT WE BELIEVE

What, then, are the principles that define America? Although the concept sounds lofty, the principles themselves are actually not complicated.

The authors of the Declaration of Independence, in announcing to the world why the United States separated from England and became an independent nation, put it succinctly: All people are created equal under the law; they are born with natural or "inalienable" rights that no government can take away; the sole purpose of government is to secure these rights; government only gets its just power from the consent of the governed; and when any government abuses those powers, the people have a right to alter or abolish it. The Constitution arranged a system of government designed to protect those principles and empower the people to be the sovereign guardians of their own future. Almost two-and-a-half centuries later, those are still the principles that define America and Americans.

The American culture embodies those principles in a way that applies to an endless array of issues, and across a vast continent now inhabited by 330 million people. The principles remain the same: freedom, equality, unalienable rights, limited government, personal responsibility, rule of law, free enterprise, private property, and mutual defense.

However self-critical Americans tend to be, most still understand the uniqueness and exceptionalism of this system. A *Washington Post* "General Social Survey" in 2014 found that 84 percent of US residents would rather be a citizen of America than any other country in the world. Why is that? How do Americans see themselves?

A few years ago, the Vernon K. Krieble Foundation commissioned a major national survey to find out how Americans view their government system and their responsibilities as citizens. Like almost all civic-related surveys in recent years, some of the results were shocking, especially in revealing how poorly Americans understand their own history and government processes. Further, it was stunning that, by a forty-point margin, Americans felt that they were less free than they had been just five years earlier. There was a strong view that government encroachment was getting worse very quickly.

Nevertheless, there were very encouraging aspects to the survey. Most Americans understand that power belongs to the people, not the government; most understand the Tenth Amendment; and most know what *e pluribus unum* really means. Perhaps most encouraging, by a twenty-two-point plurality, people believe "Rights come from the Creator, and the Constitution was written to limit government's ability to violate those rights," not that "Rights come from the government and were granted by the Constitution." Still, many Americans seem to be forever demanding more "rights," as if the government could bestow them at will. They view services ranging from on-time buses to prescription drugs not as things to be worked for and earned, but as "rights" or even "entitlements."

In fact, possibly the most puzzling symptom of America's memory loss is that most people still profess to believe in key principles, while their own voting behavior shows otherwise. To better understand this apparent contradiction, the Vernon K. Krieble Foundation commissioned "The Word Doctor," Frank Luntz, to conduct a series of dial-session focus groups in various cities to dive deeper into the survey results and attempt to find out how much people understand about their duties as citizens.

The results were profoundly disappointing. Most Americans actually do believe the "responsibilities" of citizenship are more important than "rights," which was encouraging. But when asked to name those responsibilities, virtually no participant in any focus group in any city could articulate anything more profound than being a good neighbor, recycling, attending PTA meetings at the school, obeying the law, paying taxes, and other such mundane everyday activities.

In these sessions, Luntz followed up with quotations from America's founders, explaining that the simple duties of citizenship were, first, to defend freedom against all threats, and second, to pass it along unhindered to the next generation. Sadly, not only had very few attendees ever heard that sentiment, many disagreed with it. Defending freedom, they said, was the government's job, not theirs. When he asked what if the government itself was the threat to freedom, very few had any answer, and certainly not that it would be their own personal duty to do something about it. We are responsible for these results. Our civil institutions are failing us.

The Luntz sessions also revealed that most attendants had little idea about the appropriate role for government. For example, respondents to the national survey were asked which best describes the power of the federal government, as designed in the Constitution:

A. The federal government can do whatever is necessary to improve the well-being of the people, as long as Congress passes the bill and the President signs it.
B. The federal government can only do those things that are specifically authorized in the Constitution.

Significantly more people thought the first sentence was correct, not the second. Worse yet, 20 percent of respondents thought the Constitution does not specify federal powers at all, leaving Congress and the President free to do whatever they want.

They were completely unaware that in the Constitution, all rights not specifically granted to the federal government reside with "the states and the people." This comes straight from the Ninth and Tenth Amendments in the Bill of Rights.

One of the primary foundational principles of the American republic is that of limited government, yet a majority of Americans apparently no longer believe there are any limits to what government can or should do. No wonder there is virtually nothing left which is considered "none of the government's business."

EQUALITY

America's first founding principle is equality. The Declaration of Independence, in describing the "truths" that "we hold to be self-evident," mentions equality first. That is, that all people are equally free by nature. Each has a free mind, and each has an equal right to freedom. That means we are all born with the same opportunity, not that we will necessarily achieve the same outcomes in life. Protecting that equal opportunity is a primary responsibility of government.

In theory, most Americans still strongly believe that. In the national survey mentioned earlier, two opposing views of American society were spelled out, in terms that expressed the bias of both sides. The first statement was:

> In America, we should not let the government pick winners and losers. We should not single out special groups that divide our country based on race, or belief, or origin, or any such traits for special treatment. We are one nation, united under the law that allows everyone to succeed."

The second viewpoint was:

> In America, it is appropriate for us to use government as an instrument of social progress to establish equality. Through programs like affirmative action, we can and should rectify past injustices and create a level playing field so that opportunity is available for all, not just some.

Given the choice between those two emotionally-charged views that are commonly expressed in today's politics, most people recognized the first as the correct statement of principle, by nearly a 2-1 margin. So, most Americans believe in the importance of equality, at least in the abstract, and they instinctively know that special deals for special groups violate that principle.

Despite that almost universal view of the founding principle that "All men are created equal," however, the American system of government, at all levels, has evolved into an endless array of special deals for preferred groups. That's why farmers can hire an unlimited number of immigrant laborers, but hotels cannot. It's why some people pay a higher percentage of their income in taxes than others. It's why wind and solar generators get different subsidies than gas or coal plants. It's why taxpayers subsidize cotton and corn, but not fruit and vegetables. It's why Medicare covers canes, but not hearing aids. It's why drivers of electric cars get a tax credit not available to regular car drivers. The list is almost endless.

Because Americans have not always lived up to the ideal of equal rights, equal justice, and equal opportunity for all, they have tried to make things right by creating special categories of people referred to as "disadvantaged" by virtue of their race, color, ethnic origin, gender, or some other characteristic. Such programs have good intentions. But in the long term they are destructive to the principle of equality.

For example, magnet schools serve many Connecticut communities with primarily black and Hispanic students. To try to ensure racial integration, rules were adopted requiring at least 25 percent of new students to be white or Asian. One school in New Haven had to close because it could not meet those requirements, and in Hartford, black and Hispanic students have been turned away. A brave group called the Connecticut Parents Union sued the state because its enrollment standards discriminate. Discriminating against any group is wrong, because it misses the greatest lesson of the American civil rights movement, as articulated by Martin Luther King, Jr., that people should "not be judged by the color of their skin, but by the content of their character." That may be the most elegant expression of America's first principle.

Offering some people special treatment in school admissions, hiring, promotion, or contracts, necessarily requires treating others unfairly. In America, people are supposed to succeed based on their merits as individuals, not their membership in some protected category. More than any other single trait, that is what makes America unique and special. Equality does not mean everyone will achieve the same results, but that they all should have the same opportunity to try.

A prime example of special treatment for certain chosen groups exists in nearly every state government, and in many local governments. It is euphemistically called "economic development." That generally means providing publicly financed incentives for some businesses that are unavailable to others. The ostensible purpose is to attract businesses to a community that needs more jobs, and incentives range from tax discounts to free real estate.

In Parker, CO, there were two wonderful little tack shops that catered to local horse owners. But the local economic development council offered tax breaks to lure a national chain to the town, and the big store put both local shops out of business. The incentives attracted jobs by enticing a new business, but at the expense of people who had lived there for years. Everyone understands the need for more jobs, and these deals often sound great at a ribbon-cutting ceremony. But, in the long term, they undermine the principle of equality and diminish the entire community.

Another example of market-distorting government programs is farm subsidies, which today cost taxpayers between $20 billion to $30 billion a year, mostly for corporate growers of wheat, corn, soybeans, rice, and cotton. Almost all of the money goes to corporations and wealthy people who own most of America's modern farms. One study found fifty billionaires on the *Forbes* list of the richest Americans, who had received farm subsidies. That is welfare for people who clearly don't need it. More to the point, the government has no business shelling out hard-earned tax dollars to support special groups in *any* industry.

The principle of equal treatment under law has been devastated by government's reaction to the 2020 coronavirus pandemic, especially by dictates about who can meet, who can open their businesses, and who can travel. A governor dictating that violent protests are acceptable, but church meetings are not, is the most direct example of the emasculation of America's first principle: equality.

Americans should be much more vigilant in guarding that principle. Most people probably do not realize how extensive taxpayer-funded subsidies really are. They would quickly find that taxpayers provide billions in subsidies (direct or indirect) to giant corporations like General Motors, Google, Goldman Sachs, Dow Chemical, Disney, and even retailers like Walmart, Abercrombie & Fitch, and Bed Bath and Beyond. Subsidies are intended to help particular industries and to encourage particular behavior. But they can only encourage one by discouraging another, and they threaten not only the economy, but the essential foundation of equality.

UNALIENABLE RIGHTS

American citizens' most important rights are inherent and "unalienable" because they don't come from government. There are certain natural rights that all people are born with, such as the right to life, liberty, and the pursuit of happiness. Every human has these rights, and the main purpose of government is to guarantee them.

Consider the debate over gun control that seems to follow all high-profile shootings. Americans should always ask themselves a simple question: do they have the right to defend themselves, or do they need government's permission to do so? If government banned all guns and somehow found the ability to rid the landscape of all firearms, would people still have the right to defend themselves, their property, and their families? Of course. The right of self-defense is a natural right possessed by all people, as the framers said. It is a right no government can legitimately take away, because it was not given by any government. People are born with that right, just as they are born with the right to life and the right to freely pursue their own happiness.

However unjustly governments may sometimes operate, the

American principle is that such natural rights cannot be forfeited except by due process of law, as a result of conviction in a duly constituted court operating under strict guidelines designed to protect the rights of the accused.

Sometimes the American system has strayed far from that ideal. Consider the now-common policy known as "civil asset forfeiture," which is an affront to the very foundations of American democracy. Convicted criminals obviously should not be able to keep ill-gotten wealth. But under this policy, police often seize property from people who have not been charged with a crime, much less convicted. If police merely suspect something was acquired illegally, they can take it under the justification of civil asset forfeiture. It has become a regular funding source for police departments. According to a 2014 report by the American Civil Liberties Union, American citizens lost more property to police than to burglars. People who want their property returned must prove in court that they obtained it legally, a complete reversal of the age-old principle that a person is innocent until proven guilty. Among other important protections, the Bill of Rights protects us against illegal searches and seizures. Governments may violate those rights, but such violations are unjust, and unconstitutional. The citizens, in whose hands rests the power to stop such abuses, should not tolerate them.

One of the most cherished rights is free speech, guaranteed by the First Amendment. Yet it is frequently threatened, especially on campuses across the country where administrators try to ban speech with which they disagree. They call it "hate speech" or claim it is "offensive" to some, but that misses the most important point of the First Amendment. Such protections are not needed for speech with which everyone agrees, or speech which offends nobody. College officials, of all people, should recognize that exposure to only one side of an issue is brainwashing, not education. That is counter to the very purpose of higher education, and should offend everyone.

The free speech protection clause was necessary to protect speech with which the majority disagrees. There is no such thing as the right not to be offended. People have the natural, unalienable, right to speak their mind, whether their opinion is popular or not. That is why such rights are called unalienable. They cannot be infringed under the Constitution.

A Congressman named Matthew Lyon was indicted for writing a letter to an editor criticizing the President. He was put on trial, fined $1,000, and sentenced to four months in jail. That was in 1800, and the law under which he was prosecuted was quickly repealed when Americans realized what a threat it was to their constitutional rights. But that didn't settle it forever. In 2015, the Federal Communications Commission held public hearings to discuss how to regulate online political speech, on websites like YouTube and blogs like the Drudge Report. Those hearings were a reminder that freedom is as insecure today as ever, and it is still the duty of all citizens to defend it.

PERSONAL RESPONSIBILITY

The American ideal is based on a belief that common people can govern themselves. People can take care of their own needs, not remain dependent upon a king, a government, or anyone else to provide for themselves and their families. That core principle is perhaps easiest to understand and express but may be the most difficult to live by.

A popular blogger in England, Matt Hopkins, who was born and raised in Texas, writes that:

> When the rest of the world looks in on America and judges its politics, its lack of universal healthcare, its liberal gun laws and so on, it does so without fully understanding a truly American virtue: *self-reliance*. To be self-reliant and independent is a necessary attribute for survival when you are a frontier nation, as America has been for most of its history. [...] You should then combine this with the healthy distrust of government that is taught to every American student from an early age through history and folklore. The United States of America emerged from a revolution against

an oppressive and restrictive British government [...] and it is woven into the fabric of American culture.

A graduate student at DePaul University expressed it in his thesis as a series of "values and principles rooted in individualism, self-actualization, and self-reliance where people are able to fulfill their own destiny, be self-reliant, and believe in the promise that through hard work and perseverance life can be different and better." Americans still regularly tout their self-reliance as a national badge of honor. But do they really mean it? A young woman recently complained to me that her rights were being violated because her unemployment benefits had run out. She was angry despite living in subsidized housing and on food stamps. She didn't want to find work and felt she had a right to continue living off other people's taxes. Many people now think of a college education, health care, and retirement benefits as rights. In fact, those are responsibilities. This way of thinking is symptomatic of national amnesia, because so many people have forgotten the difference. The founding documents outline the right of all people to pursue happiness, not to receive a good life for free from others.

Personal responsibility is still alive and well in some quarters. When a bridge on the island of Kauai washed out, the state government developed a two-year plan to replace it, at a cost of $4 million. The problem was that an entire community, completely dependent upon summer tourism, could not survive being out of business for two years while tourists had no access to that part of the island. So, community leaders decided to take responsibility for their own situation. They raised local money, pooled their resources, and did the job themselves—in only eight days. Too often, Americans expect government to deal with problems they could deal with themselves. The belief in personal responsibility is part of what makes Americans exceptional. They believe in limited government because they believe in self-government.

Governments, especially at the local level, do not make that easy. A friend recently replaced some windows with more energy-efficient windows, thinking she would save on energy bills, and be a responsible citizen. She quickly found out that even something as simple as replacing a window requires a permit from the county, and the fees that go with it. Building permits were originally for public safety; no one wants buildings to collapse. But, too often, such permits are not really about safety. They are about revenue for the town or the county. Some advocates may want to protect her from an installation that may not save as much energy as she wanted. But isn't that really her responsibility? There are many proper and appropriate roles for government. That would include protecting the people from foreign invaders, not from drafty windows.

Such permitting requirements frequently reach the level of absurdity in attempting to protect people from themselves. In homes across the country, doorknobs are a standard three feet from the floor. But a friend of mine was told she had to replace the doorknobs throughout her entire house with knobs four feet from the ground, because she had an indoor swimming pool, and that is a common requirement for pool rooms, even where there are no children. She was told that was because a toddler might enter her house and drown. Since the pool, which could not be seen from the street, was nonetheless called an "attractive nuisance," she would be liable if such a thing happened.

At a horse property I owned in Colorado a few years ago, I was informed that if a child pets a horse on my property and gets bitten—even if he was trespassing, even if the property was posted, even if he had to go through a gate to get there—I could be legally liable for damages, not the owner of the horse, or the parents of the child! In both of these situations, the liability is sheer nonsense. It should be obvious to any reasonable observer that a child wandering around someone else's property is the responsibility of his parents. Kids occasionally do silly things and get hurt; that is part of growing up. And it ought to be part of learning personal responsibility.

One Connecticut couple decided to let their kids walk home from school alone every day, like many of us did growing up. But nowadays people are so worried about over-protecting children that somebody called the police, and the parents were charged with a crime. These parents are fighting back. They are part of a new movement called free-range parenting, an effort to raise future independent adults. Children need to feel safe, but good citizenship also requires that they become self-reliant. America only remains free if citizens take responsibility for themselves and their children, not rely on the government. Do people really want free-range chickens but cooped-up kids?

As the Covid virus hit these shores, all of these issues reemerged. Many wanted to operate on a very rigid risk structure where kids, even when they were not at any serious risk from Covid, were deprived of in-class learning, socialization with other students, and supervised instruction. Kids were the victims of the Covid overreaction and in many states, the shutdowns were militant and harsh.

Even state governments often try to get in the parenting business. In 2018, the New York legislature considered a bill to require manufacturers to make detergent pods look "less appetizing." It was an over-reaction to the "Tide Pod Challenge," in which a few teenagers filmed themselves pretending to eat the colorful pods. About eighty teenagers reportedly tried it, which is dangerous. But, so are hundreds of other household products that are not intended to be eaten. Yet nobody was proposing to ban shampoo, paint, or oven cleaner. Such problems require the diligent attention of parents, not politicians. Government can ban products, but it cannot mandate common sense. Legislators cannot be parents for everyone and should not try to be parents for anyone.

Legislators apparently did not get that memo in Michigan, either. They spent weeks debating a bill that would pressure fast-food restaurants to stop offering "happy meals" with gender-specific toys. There were committee hearings about the cultural effects of giving kids little race cars or dolls. Legislators bloviated about the practice of asking parents if they wanted the happy meals for boys or girls, possibly leading to identity crises, or worse. Examples were made of McDonald's and Burger King, but those are both private companies. The deals they make with their customers are private exchanges and none of the government's business. Surprisingly, not a single witness questioned whether there was any proper role for government in the issue.

Americans need to conquer this national memory lapse and learn once again to rely on the personal responsibility of citizens, who either act responsibly, as most people do, or face the consequences of their own choices. If Americans believe ordinary people can govern themselves, they must learn to do so, and stop relying on government for everything.

LIMITED GOVERNMENT

America's belief in limited government only works if its people believe in self-government. The founders did not think people were perfect, nor did they naively assume a large nation could prosper without government. They were no more anarchists than today's Americans. But they had a healthy skepticism of the abuses caused by too much power in the hands of unaccountable officials. They were also well-read students of history with a keen understanding of the limits of human nature.

That is why James Madison wrote that:

> If Men were angels, no government would be necessary. If angels were to govern men, neither external nor internal controls on government would be necessary. In framing a government which is to be administered by men over men, the great difficulty lies in this: you must first enable the government to control the governed; and the next place, oblige it to control itself.

That was the primary purpose of the Constitutional convention in 1787; namely, to devise a system of government that was powerful enough to govern a far-flung and diverse nation, yet with strict limits on its own authority to usurp the rights of its people. The way to do that, the framers of the Constitution decided, was to specifically list the powers of government, and to reserve to the states and the people all the powers not listed.

Nearly two decades later, after administrations of both parties, President Jefferson still defined those limits in clear terms: "A wise and frugal government, which shall restrain men from injuring one another, which shall leave them otherwise free to regulate their own pursuits of industry and improvement, and shall not take from the mouth of labor the bread it has earned. This is the sum of good government."

In the years since then, Americans have all but forgotten the concept of leaving people free to regulate their own pursuits.

Today, whenever something terrible happens, people want to make sure it never happens again, so they make new rules, without even pausing to think about whether regulations threaten even more important principles. Government has become a maze of regulations that saps the ability to run businesses, hire people, use private property, or just earn a decent living to support families. This overreach runs the gamut from silly to business-destroying.

Consider the experience of entrepreneurs like Steve Jobs and Jeff Bezos. Jobs and his friends built the first fifty Apple computers in a California garage. Bezos started an online bookstore in his Washington garage. Today Apple and Amazon are two of the world's largest companies. Disney, Google, Harley-Davidson, and hundreds of other famous companies were started by dreamers in their garages. There are 38 million home-based businesses in the US today, earning more than $400 billion a year. But not in Milwaukee! Businesses in garages are so restricted as to be essentially illegal there. Home businesses cannot have any employees, any customers, or take any deliveries. So much for the concept of limited government.

In many parts of America, elected officials simply do not see any reason for their power to be limited. In fact, they more often assume if they were elected to lawmaking bodies they must make laws, whether new ones are needed or not.

Many of us share memories of eating ice cream in the park,

one of the great pleasures of summer. But in 2016, the city council in Boulder, CO, banned ice cream as an option for vendors in local parks. Apparently, the ice cream bars that were being sold came in larger sizes, and had higher sugar and fat content, than was allowed under the city's latest nutrition guidelines. Those rules applied to all ice cream, but also to nuts, chips, packaged fruits, cereal, cookies, pudding, and all other snacks. Should city governments even have "nutrition guidelines?" Or should people decide for themselves when and where they want to enjoy ice cream? The only good news is that the measure was later repealed.

That is no more of an overreach than the town of Blythe, CA, deciding it should be illegal to wear cowboy boots if you don't own at least two cows. Or the Denver law that makes it illegal to lend a vacuum cleaner to a neighbor. You might think such laws were always passed for some reason someone thought wise at the time. But in fact, many of them are inappropriate *now* because they were inappropriate *then*. The vacuum cleaner law had nothing to do with any public health or safety issue. It was an attempt to make everyone *buy* their own vacuum cleaners, the result of lobbying by the stores that sold them.

There are "collectors" on the Internet who compile lists of silly and antiquated laws that are still on the books. Many of them sound so pointless that they are humorous, like the old Hartford law that prohibits a married couple from kissing on Sundays. But in the larger sense, they were never really funny; they were inappropriate overreaches on the part of government officials who lacked the most basic understanding of the proper role of government. It doesn't really matter how old or new such laws are. It was never the government's business to decide when married couples can kiss, what kind of footwear they choose, whether they loan their vacuum to neighbors, or eat ice cream in the park.

Those are local and seemingly harmless examples. But the harm they do to the essential American principle of limited government is dangerous to overlook. It is the same overreaching arrogance of government that leads a federal agency to assert its authority to regulate isolated "wetlands" on private property, which has resulted in massive fines and jail time for numerous citizens, even though nothing in the Constitution gives the federal government such authority.

To the extent that Americans have forgotten their principles, they are getting the government they have asked for. They are consenting to these abuses of power by their inaction, and often by their votes.

RULE OF LAW

America has always been called a nation of laws, not men. That means it is not governed by elites, but by rules voluntarily adopted by its citizens. No government official and no citizen is above the law or immune from its reach. But today, the laws themselves have been superseded by a tsunami of regulations that have never been approved by the citizenry. People tend to think of federal agencies when the idea of "overregulation" is mentioned, because of the attention always given to rules from the Environmental Protection Agency, or the Occupational Safety and Health Administration, or the Federal Trade Commission, among many others.

As onerous as those agencies and their job-killing rules can be, they pale by comparison with state and local governments, where more than 6.1 million restrictive regulations are documented. In California alone, for example, the Code of Regulations in 2019 contained 395,129 restrictions and 21.2 million words. The Mercatus Center at George Mason University, which analyzes regulations and their impact on business, says it would take 1,176 hours, or more than twenty-nine weeks, for an ordinary person to read them all, much less understand and comply with them. The building code, as one example, has 75,712 restrictions. There are also massive regulatory codes affecting industrial facilities, natural resources businesses, motor vehicles, banking and investment, health care, professions and vocations, housing, and scores of others, all at the state level. Even a small state like Connecticut has more than 96,000 restrictive regulations, and America's least regulated state, South Dakota, has more than 44,000.

The point is not that these regulations are unneeded or unwise, though many, if not most, are. The point is that they were never adopted by the constitutional process, yet they have the force of law. Elected officials never voted on them, and they were not signed into law by governors. They skirt the rule of law and undermine the system America's framers designed specifically to ensure that government exercised its powers only by the consent of the governed.

FREE ENTERPRISE

America's economic system is based on private ownership of property and businesses, and on the ability of free people to be in whatever business they want. It is the opposite of socialism, under which government owns the property and businesses, controls production and consumption, and allocates resources, goods, and services. It is frequently called "capitalism," a pejorative term coined by Karl Marx because it conjures mental images of money and banks, which to him sounded evil. In fact, it is simply free enterprise, one of America's most essential freedoms. Indeed, even before Marx, the French writer Pierre-Joseph Proudhon, asked the question "What is property?" and answered, "Property is theft" (*La propriété, c'est le vol!*). But if people own property, who did they "steal" it from? The people who owned it before? If that is true, didn't the earlier "owners" "steal" it, too?

The "capitalist system" is really a misnomer. It isn't really a "system" at all, since that term implies a set of rules and a carefully defined process. It is simply freedom: the freedom to be in whatever business or whatever job one chooses, to earn whatever one can, and spend the proceeds however one chooses. No government decides what job fits particular individuals, and in America people do not require permission from government to work, buy a house, move to a different place, or even change careers.

That is one of the bedrock principles underpinning American democracy. But, as with other principles, Americans are quickly forgetting why it matters, as illustrated by the 2019 Gallup Survey showing 43 percent of Americans think socialism would be "a good thing" for America. The survey also shows that most people have little understanding of socialism. About 25 percent think it is about "social equality," and only 17 percent associate it accurately with government control over the means of production. The vast majority of people who think they support socialism have no idea what it is: absolute government control of every aspect of the economy. They have simply forgotten that piece of history.

No wonder American citizens increasingly grant government more and more control over the economy, even deciding who can be in various professions. In the 1950s, about 5 percent of American workers needed a state license to do their jobs, but today almost 30 percent do. It has long been understood that there is a state interest in protecting public health and safety, and nobody wants to be operated upon by an uneducated surgeon, nor to have their house burned down because of shoddy work by an untrained electrician. But today, many states require similar training, education, certification, and licensing for locksmiths, ballroom dance instructors, hair braiders, manicurists, interior designers, upholsterers, and many more, whose jobs have nothing to do with public health and safety. There is no legitimate public interest in regulating entry into those professions. They are typically about revenue for the state and about limiting competition for existing businesses, which are both inappropriate roles for government.

Central to the operation of free enterprise is the related policy of free markets. Americans have historically believed in open and free trade, where individuals and businesses may buy from, and sell to, whomever they wish. The role of government is to protect free markets against unfair competition or trade practices that threaten freedom. That includes unfair trade practices both internationally and domestically, because the government has a legitimate role in preserving free enterprise.

There should be no question about the morality of the system based on freedom, especially as opposed to that based on the force of government. Yet Americans are continually bombarded with messages about profit being somehow immoral. If the profits are large, they are said to be "windfall profits," "excessive profits," or just plain greed. Such thinking misses, or purposely ignores, the very simple reason free enterprise works. That is, nobody gets rich selling something nobody else wants.

In order to make money, a business must offer something that is of value to someone else, filling someone's need. Whether that is goods or services, the price is simply determined by how badly one needs something, and how much someone is willing to pay for it. So, a business making healthy profits only does so by supplying something customers want or need. They cannot make money any other way in a free market. That is the mutual benefit of free exchange.

Those benefits can be significantly hindered by the inappropriate intervention of government rules, especially those that significantly alter the availability, quality, or price of goods and services. And that, unfortunately, includes almost all government regulations, because they virtually all have that effect. Intervention in the economy, to some degree, is thought necessary by most modern Americans, but regulations are, by definition, limits to freedom. They should be adopted carefully, guardedly, and rarely. That is not the case today. Regulations are promulgated by the thousands every year in response to some demand from a public that has forgotten the value and importance of free enterprise.

In fact, the Code of Federal Regulations, the compilation of all federal executive branch rules, now runs more than 180,000 pages. The Mercatus Center says those federal regulations represent more than 1.07 million restrictions on business activity, all of which individuals and businesses are expected to understand and follow in order to remain compliant with the law. It is not possible for any business in America to do that.

During the coronavirus epidemic, it was quickly learned that in order to move effectively to develop a vaccine, to provide testing and other critical supplies, to allow doctors to practice their profession, regulations had to be short-circuited. What better example can there be of how regulations are stifling economic progress and the health of American citizens?

It is impossible not to conclude that Americans have forgotten the concept of leaving people free to regulate their own pursuits.

PRIVATE PROPERTY

Protection of private property is among the most important of America's founding principles. There are exceptions designed to keep people from damaging their neighbors, communities, or environment, but in general governments may not dictate what people can and cannot do in their own homes and businesses, nor prevent the full enjoyment of their private property. The ability to own property, and prosper from its use, is at the very heart of the American Revolution and the self-governmental system that emerged from it. In fact, it is often said that property is the essential right, a prerequisite to all the others.

America's founders were highly educated scholars who studied the writings of the world's most important thinkers, and nearly all of them credited John Locke with the essential theories of the Declaration of Independence. America's revolution erupted from an era of tyranny, repression, rebellion, and civil war that tore Europe apart. The world's top philosophers and writers published numerous books and pamphlets throughout the seventeenth century, and Locke was the most influential of them all. Thomas Jefferson ranked him atop the "most important" thinkers on liberty. So did Thomas Paine, George Mason, James Madison, Benjamin Franklin, and John Adams, all of whom read and studied Locke's major writings.

From Locke came the essential concepts behind several key components of the American Declaration of Independence: representative government, rule of law, the right to rebel, and especially, the idea that government is obligated to protect people's life, liberty, and property. His "Second Treatise Concerning Civil Government" contained ideas that were considered so radical in his day that Locke was never able to sign his name to it. John Hancock, Thomas Jefferson and fifty-four others did, though, in Philadelphia in 1776.

The right to property was key to the colonists' debates over the Declaration of Independence, because violations of that right were among the worst abuses of the British Crown. Locke explained that people legitimately turned common property into private property by mixing their labor with it, which improved its value and created an unalienable property right. His work established that private property is essential to freedom:

> Every man has a *Property in* his own *person*. This nobody has any right to but himself. The *labor* of his body, and the *work* of his hands, we may say, are properly his. The great and *chief end* therefore, of men's uniting into commonwealths, and putting themselves under government, *is the preservation of their property.*

It was, in the terms of today's politics, a bipartisan opinion, shared by leaders on both sides of the "aisle." James Madison led the Democratic-Republic faction in the first Congress, and wrote, "Government is instituted to protect property of every sort [...] This being the end of government, that alone is a just government, which impartially secures to every man, whatever is his own." Federalist John Adams agreed, "The moment the idea is admitted into society, that property is not as sacred as the laws of God, and that there is not a force of law and public justice to protect it, anarchy and tyranny commence."

When the Bill of Rights was added to the Constitution, the importance of property was further highlighted in the Fifth Amendment: "No person shall be [...] deprived of life, liberty, or property, without due process of law; nor shall private property be taken for public use, without just compensation."

How far America has strayed from that bedrock principle. Today, governments routinely deny people the use of their property for a variety of reasons that would have been unimaginable just a few years ago. People are denied the right to build because of wetlands; restaurants are prohibited from allowing smoking sections; zoning ordinances prevent all but the government-proscribed use of land; certain types of fences are required in some places and prohibited in others. These are just a few of the thousands of examples, but they all have one thing in common: they all restrict the use of private property.

HOW COULD WE FORGET?

My home state of Connecticut was long considered a bastion of freedom. Even today, everywhere people drive in Connecticut, they are reminded that they live in the "Constitution State." They know that because the phrase appears on the license plates of more than 1.5 million cars in the state. But *every* state has a constitution. Why is that on Connecticut's license plates?

Although Connecticut's leaders were instrumental in the Constitutional process that followed the American Revolution, this is not just ancient history. Its people remained proud of this connection as recently as 1959, when the legislature designated "The Constitution State" as the official motto, and 1978 when they required the phrase to be on all the license plates. But why did they select "Constitution State" instead of the common but unofficial nickname, "Nutmeg State," or the popular references to the historic Charter Oak?

If you notice the license plates used elsewhere, you'll see that many states want to be known for various geographic features: the mountains in Colorado, the bay in Massachusetts, the Great Lakes in Michigan, or the ocean in Rhode Island. Others proudly feature their noted products: peaches in Georgia, potatoes in Idaho, silver in Nevada, or Wisconsin's "Dairyland." Some states use license plates to promote tourism, as in Florida's boast of sunshine, Alaska's "Last Frontier," Montana's "Big Sky," or New Mexico's "Land of Enchantment."

A few states mention their history on license plates, as Illinois's

"Land of Lincoln" or Delaware's "First State." But only three use license plates—arguably the most visible space available—to remind people about important values and principles. New Hampshire and South Carolina use their famed mottos, "Live Free or Die," and "While I Breathe, I Hope." But Connecticut alone uses this tool to remind citizens of their history as home of the world's first written Constitution; not to some vague dream, or to a defiant line in the sand, but to the actual process by which a free people govern themselves.

We need a re-appreciation of our principles and freedoms that are so unique in the world today.

Until very recently, state leaders have always understood Connecticut to be a bastion of freedom, independence, and self-government. When this phrase is used today to describe Connecticut, some people actually laugh. But in the dictionary, a bastion is "an institution, place, or person strongly defending or upholding particular principles." That is the very heart of Connecticut's proud history.

Connecticut's connection to constitutional government goes back even earlier than the US Constitution. In fact, within a few years of the King's original grant of the colonial charter, Connecticut leaders met to outline the rules by which they would govern themselves. The resulting "Fundamental Orders of 1638/39" are now said to be the first written constitution in human history. As Simeon Baldwin, a former Chief Justice of the Connecticut Supreme Court, explained, "Never had a company of men deliberately met to frame a social compact for immediate use, constituting a new and independent commonwealth, with definite officers, executive and legislative, and prescribed rules and modes of government, until the first planters of Connecticut came together for their great work."

By the time debates began in 1787, about how America's new Constitution should be written, Connecticut already had 140 years of experience in the matter. That's why Connecticut's leading statesman, Roger Sherman, became a leader in the Constitutional Convention. He was the primary broker of "the Connecticut

Compromise," that resulted in a bicameral Congress, with a population-based House, and a Senate with two representatives per state. He knew a purely democratic system based on population would render little Connecticut completely powerless.

The same debate erupted over the process for electing a president, and Sherman helped devise the Electoral College to ensure small states like Connecticut had a voice. Leading several other small-state delegates, he refused to go along with the idea of a direct popular vote for the president. He knew Connecticut would be outvoted every time. The people at large, Sherman warned, "will generally vote for some man in their own state, and the largest state will have the best chance."

How appalled Roger Sherman would be, that Connecticut's legislature has now rejected its own history, and adopted the "National Popular Vote Compact." It is a devious scheme to circumvent the Electoral College, and several states have approved it. In doing so, they have agreed to allocate all their electoral votes to the winner of the national popular vote, regardless of how their own citizens voted. Participation in this deceitful ruse is ironic for any small state, but for Connecticut in particular, the great Constitution State, it is disgraceful.

The Electoral College may seem outdated to some, because the outcome of elections never pleases everyone. But that system is the only reason small states like Connecticut matter at all in national elections. It forces candidates to pay attention to the less populated states. Without that, the union of all fifty states would not exist. Over half of all the votes in the country come from just nine states.

Legislatures in New York, California, and Illinois have adopted the National Popular Vote plan for obvious reasons: they would benefit because of their large populations. But, legislatures in several small states that would be effectively disenfranchised have also bought into the idea, including Maryland, Delaware, Rhode Island, Hawaii, Colorado, New Mexico, Washington, and Oregon. The only possible explanation is that the people of those states have lost their memory about why the Electoral College ever existed. It is the surest sign of America's national amnesia.

BACK TO BASICS

America's founding principles are far from outdated. They are as sound as the day they were articulated in 1776, and they do not change over the years. What has changed is that Americans have forgotten their own past, and their own moral bearings. They have so skewed the line between "rights" and "privileges" that they scarcely know the difference. They have forgotten that rights are natural, innate, and unalienable, whereas privileges are things to be worked for and earned.

In the United States, people have the right to life, liberty, and the use of their property and resources to pursue their own happiness in whatever way pleases them, so long as it doesn't injure anyone else's rights. That is all. They are not "entitled" to free services of any kind at the expense of others.

That is what separates American citizens from those of the rest of the world. As so beautifully expressed by Thomas Paine in 1783, "Our citizenship in the United States is our national character. Our citizenship in any particular state is only our local distinction. By the latter we are known at home, by the former to the world. Our great title is AMERICANS."

The 2020 coronavirus pandemic brought the problem directly into every American home. Suddenly, the erosion of our rights was no longer a philosophical concept, but a very real and very personal affront to essential human rights. If Americans believe in self-government and individual freedom, why do so few of them object when those freedoms are blatantly violated, even under the guise of public health and safety? If Americans permanently forget their principles, and fail to cure this amnesia, their freedom will fade away, lost forever to the ash heap of historical obscurity.

CHAPTER THREE

ISSUES EVOLVE, PRINCIPLES DO NOT

America is more than just a place. It is an idea and a set of principles. In America, government exists for and with the consent of the people, which was a radical concept in 1789, and one that the founders knew would require informed and responsible citizens. Americans who enjoy the privileges of a free society must help keep that freedom on course.

Voting is a vital part of every American citizen's responsibility. But vigilant citizens should also speak out when elected leaders stray from the founding principles. Every government action can, and must, be measured against those principles. That's why it is so important for citizens to understand, and remember, those principles and how the Constitution uses them to define the role of government.

That definition, and that understanding of government's legitimate role, does not change with the seasons, nor with each new Congress, nor after each election, nor even after each generation. Those bedrock principles are not different with respect to different issues. Americans either believe in equality, unalienable rights, rule of law, personal responsibility, and free enterprise, or they do not. But if the people still hold these truths as self-evident, then they apply equally to the consideration of all contemporary issues.

Immigration, taxes, foreign relations, social welfare, energy, and many other controversial issues can be examined with the same set of principles in mind. When those principles are the basis of the discussion, answers and solutions are much simpler. Here are a few examples of how contemporary issues should be viewed through that lens.

TAX POLICY

America's tax code comprises 3,837 pages of tiny print filling six books, and IRS regulations fill another twenty volumes totaling 13,880 pages. It is estimated that Americans spend more than five billion hours a year trying to understand and comply with an enormously complex set of tax rules. Congressman Don Brotzman, who served in the 1960s and 1970s, often told the story about trying to read through a certain provision in the tax code, and by the time he got to the end of a sentence he had forgotten what the beginning of it said. He went back and counted, and discovered that the sentence was 550 words long.

Shouldn't the system for funding the United States government be easy for most Americans, who pay the bill, to understand? It would be if it were based on the simple principles of America's founding documents, the Declaration of Independence and the Constitution.

Congress has created a vast network of "categories" and "classes" of taxpayers, with a bewildering array of diverse tax levels. Married couples owe different taxes than unmarried ones; small companies owe different taxes than larger ones; homeowners owe different taxes than renters; gas stations owe different taxes than barber shops; and tens of thousands of other distinctions. Many people pay no taxes at all. But one of America's first principles is that all people are created equal and are entitled to equal treatment under the law. Instead of adhering to that principle, though, America's tax laws have evolved into a vast array of special deals for special groups.

The essential ideal of unalienable rights is also contradicted by modern tax laws. Thousands of American businesses and families are deprived of significant income by high taxes that confiscate much of their earnings; for many people nearly 40 percent. Such high taxes undermine one of America's most cherished principles: the right to life, liberty, and the pursuit of happiness. For many Americans, the pursuit of happiness requires keeping the fruits of their labor to spend as they choose, or to leave to their heirs. Americans understand the need to finance government, of course, but only if taxes are reasonable, and spent for purposes agreed to by the people who pay the taxes (the consent of the governed). A tax code of almost 4,000 pages makes that impossible.

Today's tax laws are so complex partly because they are written to encourage or discourage various behaviors. That's why some businesses get cheaper rates than others, and why taxes are much higher on products like liquor and cigarettes (there are thousands of other examples) and much lower on other favored products (like wind power and electric vehicles). Such social engineering is an improper use of tax laws, because Americans believe in personal responsibility and fairness, not government control over their behavior. Americans believe in limited government, because they believe in self-government. Using tax laws to dictate what products they buy, where they live, how they travel, and what business they're in diminishes the value of personal responsibility and gives government too much control over their lives. Remember, as the Supreme Court ruled in the early days of our Republic: "the power to tax is the power to destroy."

Tax laws should not be used to hinder, or help, particular businesses, people, or legal activities. Yet the federal government now uses taxes to encourage the use of specific types of gasoline, light bulbs, building materials, appliances, and cars; to promote savings, college education, exports, economic development in some places (but not others), and donations to some charities (but not others), to name just a few. It uses taxes to discourage smoking, drinking, and investing in businesses the government doesn't like. Government was never intended to be that intrusive. The tax system's purpose should be to raise revenue for necessary government programs, while interfering with markets as little as possible. It should not be a series of penalties and benefits to guide people toward politicians' goals.

The unequal enforcement by the IRS, especially targeting political opponents of a particular administration, has squandered American taxpayers' ability to trust in the rule of law. For example, Lois Lerner, an IRS enforcement officer appointed by President Barack Obama, used and abused her powers by targeting conservative groups and donors whose politics she didn't agree with. Some officials think that is a proper role for the IRS. President Biden proposed doubling the agency's budget for that reason.

The tax laws are so complicated that even the IRS's telephone help line regularly gives taxpayers the wrong information or guidance. A set of laws and regulations far too lengthy and complex even for officials charged with enforcement to understand and apply evenly, invites corruption and abuses of power, as today's headlines clearly show. Tax laws should always be enforced by non-biased professionals who operate in accordance with simple and clearly defined rules, never relying on personal interpretation. To meet that standard, laws must be simple enough that they are clear to everyone, taxpayers and administrators alike.

Another cherished American principle is the right to pursue one's own success. For many Americans that dream includes the right to work for a living or own one's own business. When government uses the tax laws to favor one industry (such as renewable energy), but not another (such as tanning salons or tattoo parlors), it picks winners and losers and hampers the greatest economic engine ever known: free enterprise. Americans believe their success should be based on diligent work, not the whims of politicians. Taxes are supposed to collect needed revenue, not determine what business people should be in, or how they go about living their day-to-day lives.

Today's incomprehensible tax laws and regulations also confuse the simple but vital American principle of free trade and open markets. Government's role is to preserve and protect free markets, not hinder them. That means all should face the same reasonable taxes, and regulations designed to protect public safety. Beyond that, the tax code should have no role but to generate revenue. The freedom to compete in business requires an equal playing field. That is crucial to the essential American freedoms guaranteed by the Constitution.

The right to private property, and the productive use of property, is another one of America's first principles. Property owners have a right to run the business of their choice, and to succeed or fail based on their ability to supply goods or services the public wants and is willing to pay for. So long as a business does not threaten the safety or property of others, tax policy should leave Americans free to engage in the businesses of their choice, and to pursue their own happiness.

Remember, because the federal government was, by design and constitutional authority, only granted limited powers, the need for federal tax collections was small and for more than the first 100 years of our nation, there was no federal income tax at all. That came in the early twentieth century at a low rate of tax but soon hit 70 percent and even 90 percent.

Finally, the first responsibility of government is to protect its citizens against danger, foreign or domestic. That means the revenue needed to pay for a strong defense system, and to finance police, fire, and the like, is essential to government's core mission. A tax system that has grown overly complex and controversial results in constant debates about high taxes, out-of-control spending, unprecedented deficits, and the unfathomable debt that threatens the country's very survival. A strong national defense depends on a strong military, *and* on a strong economy. American tax policy should fund the military and other government needs, but never be a hindrance that weakens the world's strongest economy. That weakens America.

SOCIAL SECURITY

The official national debt has now topped $30 trillion but it is actually much worse when it includes future spending on "entitlements."

When those obligations are included, the real national debt is an inconceivable $200 trillion, almost seven times the "official" national debt. The largest obligation among those entitlements is Social Security, a retirement program that is projected to reach insolvency in less than twenty years. Young Americans are trapped, forced to pay taxes over their entire lifetimes into programs that they never had a chance to vote on, and which may not be there for their own retirements.

Previous generations of Americans created programs like Social Security and Medicare on an unsound financial basis, which cannot be sustained long-term without significant reforms. They made promises that could not be kept by their own generation, and passed those costs along to the next. Congress has refused to address the problem for more than thirty years, while Americans have, until recently, been living longer. (US life expectancy declined 1.8 years in 2020, largely because of the premature deaths linked to COVID-19). Even so, entitlement liabilities have been growing and the current generation owes it to future generations to solve the problem.

Remember that America's first principle is equality. Then consider that Congress has created a system that cannot sustain itself, leaving unequal opportunity for future generations. When Social Security was created in the 1930s, the average American lifespan was about sixty-two years and Social Security was to provide supplemental income to those who lived longer than age sixty-five. But today the average life expectancy is more than seventy-nine years old, yet people are still eligible for Social Security in their mid-sixties. Thus, most Americans receive far more in payments than they ever put into the fund while working, and current retirees rely on payments from those now working. Because the American workforce is shrinking while the retirement base is growing, much of that burden is shifted to future generations in the form of trillions of dollars' worth of debt. Clearly, today's Americans are not giving future Americans the same equal opportunity for success that they themselves have enjoyed.

Millions of American workers, businesses, and families are

deprived of their full earning potential by payroll taxes that fund entitlements voted in by previous generations. Such taxes confiscate a significant portion of their earnings for benefits that many may never receive because of the financial insolvency of the program. They have no choice; the program is mandatory. That undermines the unalienable right to liberty, and the pursuit of happiness. For many Americans, the pursuit of happiness requires keeping enough of their income to plan for their retirement with adequate financial resources. Americans understand the need to provide for their retirement, but permanent "entitlement" programs like Social Security and Medicare tax generations of working people to pay for a system they never agreed to.

When Social Security was created in the 1930s, most Americans understood their responsibility to provide for their own retirement. They set up this program to insure against living well beyond what could be planned or expected. Today's Social Security system bears little resemblance to that vision of a retirement *supplement*. Many Americans still maintain life insurance, long-term health savings accounts, and other investments to provide for themselves and their families. But more and more Americans have grown entirely dependent on Social Security for most of their sustenance during their retirement years. That simply shifts the burden for their retirement onto the next generation of workers, which is irresponsible and immoral. American freedom is based on an understanding of personal responsibility. The concept of "entitlements" undermines that duty.

The most fundamental concept of America's founding was that government derives its just powers from the consent of the governed. But Social Security was created by Depression-era Americans in the 1930s, relies on mandatory payroll taxes on working people to finance direct payments to retirees, and offers workers no opportunity to decide whether to participate in a scheme most of them know is financially unsound. All of the Members of Congress who voted to create the program have long since gone, as has the generation of Americans who voted for them. That violates one of the most sacred principles of a democratic republic—the right of the people to be represented when tax decisions are made. Taxes levied by one generation on another, without periodic opportunities to reconsider, are inconsistent with one of the essential natural laws: no taxation without representation.

When government uses mandatory tax laws to confiscate a portion of everyone's earnings, promising to take care of them when they retire, Americans are deprived of one of the most important incentives for success. The right to work hard, earn a decent living, provide for one's family, and leave something behind for the next generation, is central to the very fabric of this country. Americans believe their success should be based on diligent work, not on a government that takes care of them from cradle to grave. Social Security has become a drain on America's economy and on the incentives of free enterprise. Even worse, it saddles future Americans with massive debt that compromises their ability to pursue their own dreams.

Today's Social Security system also interferes with what should be a free market. By prescribing the nature of retirement for millions of Americans, it precludes their ability to invest in other systems. That hinders the market for private retirement programs, life insurance, health savings accounts, and other systems that may provide much greater security. In fact, the government's mandatory program is completely misnamed, especially since its future is far from secure. It is nothing more than a retirement insurance program; one based on unsound financing and a business model that cannot be sustained. Worst of all, it takes billions out of the economy in mandatory payroll taxes that might otherwise be invested in private markets that could thrive, and that could provide much greater "security" for retirees.

If Social Security were viewed not as a retirement program (which it is not) but as an insurance product (which it is), it would be much more obvious how badly structured it is. Very few free customers would ever buy into such a scheme. But the freedom for businesses to compete in offering better services is hindered because the mandatory nature of FICA taxes gives the program a government-dictated monopoly, confiscating money that could be invested in better systems. That is an inappropriate role for government under the Constitution. If young workers were simply allowed to "opt out" of Social Security and put 10 percent of their paychecks each pay period into an IRA, they would retire as pension millionaires—not as government dependents.

ENERGY POLICY

Building and maintaining a prosperous economy requires substantial use of natural resources. Every aspect of American life is influenced by the people's use of resources, especially to create the energy that heats, cools, and lights their homes and businesses, and fuels their transportation, manufacturing, and food supply. Fortunately, the United States contains some of the world's largest reserves of coal, oil, gas, and other minerals, and includes many of the best locations for using the sun, wind, water, geothermal, and other "renewable" forms of energy. Yet Americans debate endlessly how, and even whether, to use these resources.

In fact, Americans frequently decide against using their own domestic resources at all, because of local environmental concerns, or the fear of global warming, or just because many believe that Americans consume too much. Founding principles are often forgotten in the passion of these debates. If applied consistently, those principles would result in a more robust and cheaper energy supply, while making the world considerably safer.

Equality is sacrificed every time government decides to promote one form of energy over another, require the use of more expensive renewables, or add to production costs through taxes and regulations. Picking winners and losers in the energy marketplace raises the cost of energy and, indirectly, of all the products Americans buy. Such increases hurt the most for those least able to pay: the poor and the elderly. Government policy, including taxes, regulations, and environmental rules, should be fair and equal for all businesses, all citizens, and all parts of the country.

The beauty of freedom—of the universal right to life, liberty, and the pursuit of happiness—is that everyone may define their own happiness and pursue it however they choose. But when the government dictates every aspect of energy policy, from where the power company gets its electricity to the kind of light bulbs consumers are forced to buy, it imposes someone else's view of happiness. That denies individual citizens and businesses their equal right to buy, sell, trade, produce, manufacture, and profit from their own pursuits. All Americans have a right to pursue their own dreams, and government interference in the marketplace (for energy or any other products or services) chips away at that "inalienable right."

Instead of offering incentives for more efficient and cleaner uses of energy, government generally imposes strict regulations, unequal taxes, mandates on companies that produce or transmit energy, and even bans many projects completely (such as pipelines, power plants, and mines). Americans who believe in self-government should not need federal agencies to determine that everyone has a "responsibility" to use energy wisely. Under the free-enterprise system, people have a self-interest in doing so, because wasting energy costs more than wise use. That incentive is far more effective than the heavy hand of government. The government can advise its citizens on wise practices, but should leave them free to make their own decisions about what energy to buy and use, and where to obtain it.

Today's federal government regulates every aspect of the design of cars, and building materials for homes and businesses, from roofs to windows, even the light bulbs used. More than thirty-five states now dictate to electric companies the percentage of power they must generate from which energy sources. This makes utility bills higher in these states; in some cases monthly bills can be twice as high because of these renewable energy requirements. They are like a secret tax. The EPA and its allies have spent years trying to impose regulations that would effectively ban the use of America's most abundant energy source (coal), while Congress has used tax dollars to subsidize others. The Constitution empowered Congress to regulate interstate and foreign commerce, in order to avoid a myriad of different trade rules in different states. That power was never intended to be used to regulate the buying, selling, and lifestyle of every American citizen in his own home.

Perhaps worst of all, many of today's energy regulations were never passed, or even debated, in Congress. Instead, they were written and enforced by executive branch agencies, which are neither elected by nor accountable to the people. Such regulations drive up the cost of goods and services for everyone, and they violate a fundamental principle that government requires the consent of the governed. Federal laws should be enacted by a vote of both Houses of Congress with the President's signature. Any other process for regulating people and their businesses violates the rule of law.

Today's overregulation of energy undermines the simple principle of free markets. Government should ensure that *all* energy sectors face the same regulations, taxes, and other rules. Beyond that, consumers have the right to decide what products or services to use. Businesses that provide what the public wants will prosper; that's how the market works. Government's legitimate role is to protect the free market, not hinder it. The freedom to compete in business requires an equal playing field, and the marketplace will decide the outcome.

The right to private property, and the productive use of property, is another of America's first principles. But the federal government owns almost a third of America, including vast energy-rich lands across the nation (mostly in the West), and severely restricts access to those resources. Federal ownership has deprived Americans of available and affordable mineral resources that are central to a prosperous economy. Worse, the government also controls energy production on private property, through restrictive regulations and punitive taxes. So long as a business does not threaten the safety or property values of its neighbors, government should leave Americans free to supply their own energy needs, in accordance with market demand. Many advocates argue, of course, that energy production does impact the value of others' property by its effects on the environment. But more often, the argument is not about neighboring properties but the theory that the use of energy itself, by the whole society, threatens the entire planet. Restricting the use of some property for that reason, while allowing continued production on other property elsewhere, is an improper role of government.

The greatest irony of today's energy policies is they threaten government's first responsibility to protect its citizens against danger. Today's world is more dangerous because of America's decades-long reliance on imported energy. Exploration and production of America's own vast resources not only enhances national security for the US, but also could help the rest of the world rely less on the Middle East and Russia. That could make the world considerably safer, by reducing conflicts throughout the Middle East, and eliminating Eastern Europe's dependence on Russia. Policies that restrict production of oil, gas, coal, biomass, nuclear or any other energy are a threat to America's national security. The United States should rely on its own resources first and foremost, and never be subject to the policy whims of foreign governments.

THE ENVIRONMENT

Nearly all Americans agree on the importance of protecting the environment, and the United States has done more to improve the environment than any nation in history. For example, most Americans don't know—because the media doesn't tell us—that the United States has reduced its carbon footprint more than virtually any nation in the world over the past decade. A *Forbes* magazine article citing the 2017 BP Statistical Review of World Energy, explained that since 2005 annual US carbon dioxide emissions have declined by 758 million metric tons, by far the largest decline of any country in the world. That almost equals the decline in emissions of the entire European Union, and stands in stark contrast to India's emissions growing by one billion metric tons, and China's by three billion.

Yet issues like clean air and water, healthy forests, climate change, and endangered species have become divisive, contentious, and partisan despite almost universal agreement on their importance.

These issues no longer lead to easy agreement, but to anger, bitterness, lawsuits, and perhaps worst of all, government steadily chipping away at freedom, and banning all sorts of human activity in the name of environmental protection, public health, and other excuses. There is a simple reason that these issues have become so divisive: Americans have forgotten and veered away from important principles.

Consider equality first. The federal government owns much of the West, but almost none of the Eastern United States. This has allowed eastern congressmen to dictate land use policies in western states. Urban representatives are trying to tell rural farmers and westerners how to plant their crops and raise their cattle. Agencies routinely pick winners and losers, deciding who can use public lands and who cannot, and enforcing environmental rules strictly in some places while ignoring them in others. But Americans believe in equal treatment for all, not special deals for special groups. Environmental protection, restoration, and improvement should always be applied fairly and equally to all businesses, all citizens, and all parts of the country.

Overregulation of land use in the name of the environment has restricted freedom for thousands of American businesses and individuals, undermining one of their most cherished principles: the right to private property. For many generations, the American Dream has included owning property, whether it is farm, a business, or just a home. Regulations that restrict activity on private property chip away at this most basic American principle. Government tends to view people as a threat to the environment, but people are part of the environment. Government policy should seek to work with property owners, not run over them.

Instead of offering incentives for environmental improvement, government often imposes criminal penalties even for small violations of complex rules. State and local governments are not trusted to protect their environment without the heavy hand of federal agencies. The American experiment was based on the idea of limited government, and self-government by ordinary people. Yet today there is a pervasive attitude assuming the environment must be protected from the American people themselves. That diminishes the importance and the value of personal responsibility. The federal government should help establish standards for a healthy environment that people and businesses can attain. Enforcement should assume that people share that desire, and leave local citizens, communities, and states free to determine how best to achieve those goals. Criminal enforcement should be viewed as the last resort, not the first choice.

Instead of encouraging freedom, though, the federal government dictates all activity on public lands, the use of all minerals, the source and content of food, the location of all energy facilities, transportation of waste, design of cars and trucks, standards for building homes, where birds and animals can live, and even whether natural substances like carbon dioxide are really pollutants. There is a legitimate government role in protecting the country from pollution and other damage, especially across state lines. But regulating every aspect of American life under the guise of "protection" is a threat to the fundamental principle of limited government. The Constitution does not give Congress, or any agency, such authority.

Like tax laws, current environmental laws are inconsistent and overly complicated, even for government officials. That invites corruption, and often results in arbitrary enforcement based on the whims of bureaucrats, or worse yet, on deals made with powerful environmental organizations or politically connected groups. That undermines public confidence in government and respect for the rule of law, and also harms the environment. Federal environmental laws should be simple and straightforward, easy to understand, and applied the same everywhere. But since the environment varies so widely in different parts of the country, most of the responsibility for protection and improvement should lie with state and local governments.

As with the previous discussion on energy policy, restrictions on legitimate business activity hinder the unalienable right to pursue happiness. Since most businesses have some impact on their environment, today's government uses that excuse to regulate nearly every aspect of many enterprises, even entire industries. Restraining the risk-taking and entrepreneurial spirit of the American people is a threat to the country's fundamental economic system. Businesses and individuals own and control most of America's environment, so public policies need to recognize the important role of landowners by focusing more on incentives and less on enforcement.

Today's overregulation of everything, from energy and manufacturing to agriculture and transportation, interferes with free trade and open markets. Businesses buy, sell, trade, and transport goods and services every day, but environmental enforcement often interrupts that process, delaying or halting important projects. The use of natural resources is necessary for a growing economy, and government can never understand, legislate, and regulate every aspect of that relationship in all places at all times because that's a function of the market. Government should provide simple standards for a healthy environment, then let the market work. Since the public cares deeply about environmental issues, responsible and sustainable businesses will always be more successful. That's how a free market works.

LICENSING AND PERMITTING

Do you need a license to reupholster a chair? In seven states, you can pay a hefty fine if you don't have one. Remember that today, nearly 30 percent of workers need a license to do their jobs. It is understandable if there is a safety issue, as with electricians or doctors. But what is the public interest in requiring licenses for barbers, hair stylists, auctioneers, or interior designers? In some states, braiding hair requires thirty-two hours of training. Americans should not need government's permission to work. Licensing and permitting requirements have grown so ubiquitous, in every state, that Americans are quickly forgetting the importance of the individual freedom that is their birthright.

In my hometown, several parents volunteered to decorate the school gym for the annual prom, just as parents all across America have done for generations. But in this case, nobody seemed aware that a permit from the local fire department was required, along with its approval of the specific decoration plan. Firemen ripped down the decorations, too late to be replaced for that year's prom. Government overreach is evident in communities of every state, even though many Americans recognize that such permits and overzealous enforcement are often more about revenue than safety. Yet, by their inaction, citizens consent to the chipping away of freedom in thousands of little ways every day.

A friend of mine has spent years in Washington, DC, and, as a history buff, is an excellent tour guide. But he had to stop giving tours of the Capitol's most famous landmarks because the government now says all tour guides must have permits. In New York City, the powerful Tour Guides Association requires a certification test, which all guides must pass to get a license from the city. The test, of course, is filled with mundane details like dates and other statistics that bore many tourists. More to the point, is it really the government's business which facts tour guides choose to tell their customers? Tour guides are no threat to public health or safety, yet in some places, you could be arrested for showing your friends around town.

America now has an official National Lemonade Day, thanks to an organization that thought such an event would be a great way to teach kids how to start, own, and operate their own business—a lemonade stand. They host events in thirty-six cities, but sadly not in hundreds of other communities where kids' lemonade stands are illegal. Of course, there are concerns about food prepared in kitchens that may not be approved by the local health department, yet such rules teach the wrong lessons. Kids are learning that government regulations, zoning laws, licenses, and taxes destroy their small businesses and discourage them from ever trying again.

Government regulation is out of control, and ironically, most of it occurs not at the Environmental Protection Agency, but at the local level. An Arizona grandmother had a problem with rats in her attic, so she asked her seventeen-year-old grandson to help. He went to the hardware store, got some wire mesh to cover the holes, and solved the problem. When his grandmother's friends heard about it, they began hiring him to help with the same problem. Earning $30 per home, he saved money for college, until the local government shut him down. They insisted he pay fees, get a commercial pest control license, and pass a forty-page chemical safety test, even though he used no chemicals. In a case such as this, an overzealous bureaucracy is much more dangerous than a teenager getting the rats out of granny's attic.

Another example of government overreach comes from Tennessee, where a pastor saw funeral homes marking up the price of caskets as much as 600 percent, which prompted him to set up shop, selling caskets much cheaper. He was immediately successful, until the state said it was illegal for anyone other than licensed funeral directors to sell caskets. He was expected to complete two years of training, spend thousands of dollars, embalm twenty-five bodies, and pass the exam. He explained that he only wanted to sell caskets, not embalm bodies, but to no avail. So, he challenged the unconstitutional law. The courts agreed with him that the state was protecting established businesses against competition, and not protecting public health or safety.

Such protectionism underlies scores of regulations in every state. Two Colorado neighbors had pet dogs and jobs requiring frequent travel. So they had an arrangement for many years, where they took care of each other's dogs when either was out of town. Then they found out they had been breaking the law all along and could face stiff fines. Like many other states, Colorado required anyone who cared for a pet to have a license and pay fees. But the law made no distinction between a large commercial kennel, and a neighbor or family member. One of these neighbors insisted that her private dealings with friends were none of the government's business. She took up the cause and convinced the state to change the law, showing the power of one dedicated citizen.

In every state, drivers with medical issues can get handicapped signs to display in their car windshields. They are cut in the shape of a hanger so they can be attached to the rearview mirror. But if you hang one in your car in Illinois, you could get a ticket, just as you can for hanging an air freshener, a parking permit, or a pair of foam-rubber dice. Illinois police pulled over 38,000 drivers in one year for hanging something on their mirrors, even the handicapped signs issued by the state. Instead of looking at what's on the mirror, they should look again at America's founding principles, and ask if the Constitution gives the government any authority to determine whether you can have an air freshener in your car.

A Wisconsin hardware store owner could no longer stay in business, so he sold his building, liquidated his inventory, and closed up shop. Then he got a $510 fine for not having a permit to go out of business! Regulations, fees, and permits make it difficult enough to stay in business. But in Milwaukee, Boston, Albany, and hundreds of other cities, you also need a permit to close your business. Those cities require an itemized inventory of all equipment and supplies, every day the business is selling anything, along with a percentage of the revenue as a fee. There is no legitimate public safety reason for what one writer calls the "sayonara tax." Businesses fail for various reasons, but do they really need government to drive the last nail in the coffin?

When Josh Spencer opened his business in Los Angeles, he called it "The Last Bookstore" because so many others had gone out of business in this digital age. But in LA, the problem is more than just online competition. That city treats used bookstores the same as gun shops. Owners need a police permit, and must hold all books at least thirty days before selling them. Each book must be stamped with a number, corresponding to records identifying the book and where it was purchased, and sellers and suppliers must be finger-printed. That applies to all books, even copies of the Constitution! Ruthless dictators may hate books, but this is America, where public officials need to spend less time regulating the Constitution, and more time reading it.

EDUCATION

Educational policy, funding, curriculum, and management are continuously debated in the halls of government, at the local, state, and federal levels. That is because the government owns most of America's schools. Why is that? Why would America's founders, with such strong beliefs in limited government and free enterprise, nevertheless think schools ought to be owned and operated by the state?

Noah Webster wrote:

> It is an object of vast magnitude that systems of education should be adopted and pursued which may not only diffuse a knowledge of sciences, but may implant in the minds of the American youth the principles of virtue and of liberty, and inspire them with just and liberal ideas of government, and with an inviolable attachment to their own country.

Most American students today, more than 50 million, attend public (government) schools. Only 10 percent attend private schools, and another 4 percent are homeschooled, though that number increases each year. In fact, a fourth of all parents now say they are considering taking their children out of public schools, amid growing concerns about the quality of state-sponsored education. Many writers, organizations, and politicians now openly wonder if public schools have outlived their usefulness. It is a tempting view, because so many public schools have forgotten their essential purpose. It needs to be reestablished.

This does not necessarily mean effective schools must be owned and managed by the state. Nor does it suggest that private and home schools fail by comparison (test scores clearly show otherwise). So, why are there *public* schools in the first place? At the time of the American Revolution, the country was full of private and home schools, turning out some of the brightest scholars the world had ever seen. Yet the founders were nevertheless intent on creating a system of state-run public schools for everyone, not just their own elite class. Why?

America's founders knew that the democratic republic they envisioned would be new, untested, and unsupported by much of the world. Indeed, the idea that ordinary people could govern themselves was laughable to most eighteenth-century nations (it still is, to many). The founders knew such a system could survive only if its people were virtuous, public-spirited, and well-educated. Breaking away from centuries of monarchy and replacing it with a system based on the rule of law, individual freedom, and personal responsibility, meant giving sovereignty itself to ordinary people, turning former subjects into self-governing citizens. That could only work if citizens understood the difference.

Although schools were plentiful in colonial America, they were attended mainly by the children of the upper classes. Lower-class children were as likely to be indentured servants, or even slaves, not students. Yet the founders envisioned a country in which all shared in the responsibility of government, so every citizen needed at least a rudimentary education. That wasn't because every child "deserves" an education, as is often said today, but because the American system of government depended on the ability, and willingness, of citizens to be involved.

That's why George Washington believed "a plan of universal education ought to be adopted in the United States." He wanted to teach "the people themselves to know and to value their own rights; to discern and provide against invasions of them; to distinguish between oppression and the necessary exercise of lawful authority." "In a Republic," Washington asked, "what species of knowledge can be equally important, and what duty more pressing on its Legislature, than [...] a plan for communicating it to those who are to be the future guardians of the liberties of the country?"

Even before the Revolutionary War ended, Thomas Jefferson had introduced a public-education bill in Virginia. He wrote that "the most effectual means of preventing [tyranny] would be, to illuminate, as far as practicable, the minds of the people at large."

That is the reason schools were to be for everyone. Even today's National Education Association recognizes,

> One of the primary reasons our nation's founders envisioned a vast public-education system was to prepare youth to be active participants in our system of self-government. The responsibilities of each citizen were assumed to go far beyond casting a vote. Protecting the common good would require developing students' critical thinking and debate skills, along with strong civic virtues. Blind devotion to the state or its leaders would never be enough. Rather, being American was something to be learned and carried out.

Note the NEA's use of the past tense. How ironic, that those very purposes have been largely removed from the curricula of modern public schools. In fact, today's education establishment is largely opposed to teaching moral values, civic virtue, and founding principles. Such concepts are considered subjective, and even offensive, by many. In 1979, economist Murray Rothbard wrote in *Education: Free and Compulsory* that the purpose of public education was not so much the three R's, but indoctrination in the "civic religion," or the values the state considers important.

Originally, the values important to the state were those needed to perpetuate itself. Indeed, it is natural for all governments to create systems to ensure their own survival. Public schools were America's primary system for doing so. Today, though, that system is losing its memory, forgetting the lessons of history, and thus failing to pass along that knowledge to future generations.

That is why only a fourth of high-school seniors today are proficient on the standardized civics exam. Scores are consistently pathetic when the National Assessment of Educational Progress tests history, civics, and geography. Even the national test required for new citizens completely ignores America's founding principles, instead testing simple memorization of names and dates. Citizens are expected to know *when* the Civil War was fought, not *why* it was fought. They must know *who* wrote the Federalist Papers, not what they are *about*.

All these problems were exacerbated in recent years as most states shut their schools for more than a year, causing real setbacks for children as they develop.

WHEN LESSONS ARE FORGOTTEN

Though America is large, powerful, and prosperous, its unique concept of self-government cannot survive if the people no longer understand and value it. The United States is losing the knowledge of what it takes for people to be truly free, just as surely as an island tribe becomes isolated by losing its knowledge of sailing. If schools are to remain public, and remain important, they must resume their vital role of teaching citizens their responsibilities.

Instead, America's public schools are laser-focused on competing with other nations to turn out better workers. They consider it a crisis that American students are falling behind the Chinese and Indians in fields like engineering and computer programming. Those are important skills, but will no longer matter if the very freedom that enables them is lost.

It is the sacred duty of all American citizens to defend their freedom against all threats, and to pass it on, undiminished, to the next generation. People are not born with an instinctive understanding of those duties; they must be taught. Public schools are failing miserably in that most important function—their very reason for existence.

~~~

CHAPTER FOUR

IMMIGRATION: IT'S NOT THAT COMPLICATED

The immigration issue is a glaring example of America's profound amnesia.

No issue in recent memory has been more divisive, polarizing, and frustrating than the never-ending discussion of illegal immigration. It has divided Republicans and Democrats along stark partisan lines, but the divisions run much deeper. Proposals to reform the nation's immigration system have also divided traditionally aligned factions: labor unions and civil rights groups, business associations and law-and-order conservatives. Administrations and Congresses of both parties have struggled with the issue for more than thirty years, unwilling to act on any reform for fear of alienating one constituency or another, paralyzed to the point of virtually ignoring one of America's most pressing issues.

Political leaders may think problems go away if ignored long enough. But our national problem with border security and illegal immigration is not going away. They are getting worse with each passing week, and the Biden administration's border policy, is a national disgrace and threat to our security. Today's dangerous world still demands secure borders, and small businesses still face labor shortages that threaten their ability to grow and create more jobs. Still, the debate raging in Washington's power circles is not really about how best to secure the borders, or how to create a safe and practical nonimmigrant worker program. It is about whether to do anything at all.

People on both sides of the southern border are growing angrier by the minute. The US and its allies and trading partners throughout the Americas sometimes treat each other more like enemies. Political leaders on both sides of the aisle continue to argue about whether the time is right for any action at all.

In 2019, politicians even spent several weeks bickering about whether the issue represented an "emergency" or a "national crisis," although both sides used precisely those terms for years. It's both! As has so often been the case, politicians are mostly jockeying for position to win the next election.

The perennial effort to make this issue seem complicated and difficult is disingenuous. It helps candidates use it as a "wedge" issue in campaigns, but never comes close to a genuine concern about the all-too-real victims of today's broken system. Those victims include both the migrants themselves, and the vast economy of American small businesses.

In truth, the issue is not that complicated. The Vernon K. Krieble Foundation has been working diligently on this issue, as one of its highest priorities, for fifteen years. That experience has proven that reasonable people discussing the issue dispassionately almost invariably find themselves more in agreement than not. In fact, it is painfully obvious what is wrong, and not terribly difficult to envision practical solutions. But that is only true among leaders who want solutions. Sadly, many of the leaders of Congress are not in that category. Instead, they seek total government control of the nation's labor market, and open borders to attract more future voters. Both are entirely inconsistent with the founding principles of America.

START WITH THE BASICS

Every issue facing America should always be viewed through the perspective of its founding principles. Its Constitutional system was set up for that very reason. The founders could not envision in the eighteenth century every issue that might someday arise (they certainly could not have anticipated today's discussion of temporary work visas), so they created a process for addressing any and all matters, in a way that protected the essential unalienable rights of the people. Even though it has worked for 240 years, today's citizens tend to make up their minds for or against an idea based on a superficial understanding of details, rather than evaluating it against those principles. That approach can easily deprive them of the most obvious answers.

Remembering America's founding principles is not difficult, because they are clearly spelled out in its founding documents: the Declaration of Independence and the Constitution. If the US is to continue to be the freest country on Earth, every legislative decision needs to fall within this framework. So, what are those core principles, as they relate to a discussion of immigration?

Americans believe in:

- Equal treatment under the law, allowing no special deals for special groups
- Limited government with defined powers, because responsible individuals can govern themselves
- Personal responsibility, not a government that cares for all its citizens' needs from cradle to grave
- Free markets, free exchange, supply and demand, and a vital private sector in which individuals are free to succeed or fail without government interference
- The rule of law, not in a massive police state controlled by government, but a means of protecting individual rights against abuses
- Secure borders which protect the national sovereignty

No immigration plan proposed in Washington in the past twenty years adheres to these principles. The worker shortage today in America is only highlighting the need for action that is in America's national interest.

Equality. The first statement of principle in the Declaration of Independence is that "all men are created equal." Equality ought to mean no special deals for special groups. Yet Congress has created a mishmash of "categories" under which guest workers and immigrants are admitted to the US, and those categories are often targeted for revisions. The result is special deals with different types of visas for people engaged in farming, health care, athletics, entertainment, or other fields the government thinks America "needs." The debate often veers off into a discussion of immigrants with special "merit," such as science, technology, engineering, and mathematics. But what authority do congressmen have to determine who has "merit" and who does not? How can they decide whose labor is "skilled" and whose labor is "unskilled?" The very existence of such categories is an affront to the first founding principle. If Americans believe in equal treatment for all, there should never be special deals for special groups.

Limited Government. Americans believe in limited government because they believe in self-government. But today the federal government not only dictates who can enter the US, but also who employers can and cannot hire and fire, how much they must pay, what qualifications they must seek, and how long a job can last. Worse, it dictates how many workers will be available for which industries, picking winners and losers among favored industries. Nothing in the Constitution gives Congress such power over such a broad segment of the economy. Immigration is a governmental responsibility, but hiring and firing workers is a function of private business.

Personal Responsibility. The government should set the rules for immigration and citizenship. But today, it also assumes authority over hiring, firing, qualifications, wages, benefits, working conditions, length of service, eating, sleeping, and even personal sanitation. The American system is based on limited government, and laws that dictate every aspect of our working relationships diminish the value of personal responsibility.

Free markets. Thousands of businesses today cannot find the workers they need, undermining one of America's most cherished principles: the right to life, liberty, and the pursuit of happiness. For many Americans, the pursuit of happiness means running a business, earning a profit, and succeeding. Laws that make it difficult to hire legal workers (even purposely limiting the available workforce with artificial quotas) hinder free enterprise. Americans believe people are entitled to the fruits of their labor, with success based on diligent work. That risk-taking, entrepreneurial spirit is curtailed when workers and employers can't find each other in a safe, legal, and workable process.

Rule of Law. Current immigration laws are inconsistent, offer no mechanism for foreign workers to get visas for US jobs, and no simple means for American businesses to find legal workers. That invites corruption and results in an underground economy that is inconsistent with the rule of law. Indeed, the systematic abuse of thousands of migrants is proof of a process operating with virtually no rules at all.

Secure Borders. The first responsibility of government is to protect its citizens against danger, so controlling the border is essential. Criminals or terrorists entering the US, masked among thousands of workers streaming across a porous border, must be filtered out by eliminating the camouflage of people simply looking for work. The strongest security comes from allowing entry only to foreign guest workers with legal permits and background checks, neither of which are readily available today. Such a system, utilizing modern technology, should be funded by employers and workers, not taxpayers. If law-abiding workers always entered through carefully controlled gates, border agents could focus on stopping everyone sneaking across the border, since only criminals would have any reason to cross illegally. Border security would be enhanced and America would be safer. Instead, the government's failure to control this situation violates its fundamental duty to "provide for the common defense" of its citizens.

HOW BAD IS IT?

No one knows exactly the number of illegal aliens in the US; estimates range between 10 and 30 million, and there are dozens of competing studies. Nor is it known how many of this number are workers or family members, how many intend to become permanent residents, how many came across the border illegally, or how many came legally but overstayed their visas. In short, the government does not know, and cannot know, very much about this large population. That fact itself is a serious problem.

The impact of this enormous labor force on the American economy is staggering. It has fueled years of public demands for better control of the borders, and to stop the use of tax money to subsidize people who break the law. Yet, as the US labor force ages and shrinks, its economy is also increasingly dependent on immigrant workers, prompting political leaders to struggle for solutions. Despite several major legislative efforts since the 1980s, no workable solution has yet emerged, partly because the entire debate is based on a false premise. In a national debate on "illegal immigration," leaders on every side of the issue miss a critically important point: the activities of most illegal aliens in this country have nothing to do with actual immigration.

The solution would be much simpler if leaders understood that the vast majority of illegal workers in the US are not here seeking citizenship, or even permanent resident status. That's why so few have taken advantage of the various offers of legal status extended from time to time. Most are workers with families to support back home, and they have every intention and desire to return home. Most are here because they cannot hope to earn as much money working at home. They are here for the money so they can feed their families, not because they want to be permanent Americans. Thus, they are not immigrants. They are often referred to as "migrant" workers, "undocumented" residents, the "unauthorized" population, or by other terms. Millions are here illegally. But the debates about "illegal immigration," and solutions proposing a "path to citizenship" fuel deep-seated concerns about amnesty, and even voting rights, for people whose only qualification is a blatant defiance of the law. However, since this is not the objective of most illegal aliens, a program providing efficient, legal, non-citizen work permits for these people could be implemented with only a few very simple changes in immigration laws.

AN UNCOMPLICATED SOLUTION

Such a simple program is the basis of a proposal the Vernon K. Krieble Foundation published several years ago, called the "Red Card Solution." It has been an important part of this discussion for more than a decade. It is supported by dozens of national leaders involved in the issue, and it offers the most practical and workable solution available. It also provides a reminder of how much easier solutions are when viewed through the lens of America's founding principles; the fundamentals that citizens cannot afford to forget.

The proposal is a market-driven, private-sector, guest-worker plan that begins with separating citizenship from guest workers. They are two different processes, with completely different goals, and should never be confused. Citizenship should be a challenge, but getting a job should be easy. This proposal clearly defines two separate paths for entry into the US, one for workers and one for people who intend to immigrate.

The implementation is simple if it relies on systems already in place, and uses people who are already good at what needs to be done:

- Empower private employment agencies to create a database for employers to post jobs, and for workers to post applications
- Match workers and jobs
- Run background checks like those done by gun shops every day

- Collect the fees from both employers and workers to pay the program's expenses
- Take photos and fingerprints
- Issue work permits in the form of "smart cards," with the required data encoded in microchips
- Workers are then free to cross the border and go to work

Consider the practicality of using the existing private sector. Businesses make their living performing these services every day, routinely putting jobs and workers together, running background checks, issuing smart cards that are impossible to duplicate, and transferring information around the world instantly. They have the ultimate motivation for speed and accuracy: profit. Both employers and employees have a strong desire to operate legally and this would finally give them the means to do so. Best of all, this system would be financed by user fees, not taxpayer dollars.

Domestic American workers would always have an advantage over foreign workers because of the fees required of employers who hire guest workers. There need be only two requirements for workers: passing the security background check, and having a self-supporting job. Such a permit would not lead to green cards or citizenship, which would be a separate process. Anyone in the world can apply for American citizenship, but possession of a temporary work permit would not give the holder any special place in that line. It would have nothing to do with citizenship or immigration. It would simply be a permit to work, nothing else.

Such a simple program would work by incentives, not coercion. That's why it would work for employers, for foreigners wanting to work in the US, for workers already in the US illegally, and for border security.

This proposal is so simple that when former Congressman John Shadegg (R-AZ) had it drafted into legislation, the bill was only twelve pages long. Contrast that with the last serious attempt at legislation in the Senate, the so-called "Gang of Eight Bill" in 2013. Its multi-billion cost was never fully estimated, the amounts of new fees assessed were never specified, and the dozens of special deals for special groups were never well understood. Yet that proposal was 867 pages long and virtually no senator claimed to have read and understood the entire bill. No wonder it proved impossible to muster the majorities needed for such landmark legislation. A simpler proposal, even one of only twelve pages, might still face opposition, but there could never be any doubt about what was in it.

THE CURRENT VISA SYSTEM DOESN'T WORK

Leaders on all sides of the debate know a new legal work program is clearly needed, one that can supply the needed workers and stabilize the economies of the US and its neighbors to the south. Virtually all agree that national security concerns must be addressed by controlling the borders. But much disagreement still exists about whether or not illegals already in the US can be persuaded to go through new steps to get documented.

Illegals already in the US, and the employers who hire them (sometimes knowingly, but often not), live in constant fear of raids, apprehension, deportation, or jail. A program enabling them to come out of the shadows and into the American system of freedom and personal responsibility is their strong desire. Several proposals in recent years have included a plan to make illegals go home, pay a fine, reapply, and reenter legally. The Bush Administration proposed this approach in 2007 and according to numerous polls, American voters strongly supported it. But it soon became clear that it would not work. Simply put, there are two very powerful disincentives that prevent most illegals from voluntary "self-deportation."

First, most of these workers do not trust the immigration bureaucracy to handle the caseload efficiently, nor should they. These workers certainly would have come legally if they could easily have done so. They came illegally precisely because the system could not legally get them to the US in an efficient and timely manner. Expecting them to return to the same government office that could not help them before is unrealistic.

Second, and even more important, artificial quotas imposed by Congress upon the number of visas issued means there will never be as many visas as workers who want them, or employers who need them. For instance, Congress limits the number of H-2B visas (for unskilled laborers) to 66,000 per year for the entire country, even though there is obviously a market for several million. As long as the number is thus limited, what illegal worker can be expected to return home and apply for a visa, not knowing whether he might be applicant number 66,001?

As long as those two powerful disincentives remain, illegals can never be expected to leave the US voluntarily and reenter legally. That is why deportation, even voluntary, has not been part of the more recent debates in Congress. It does not need to be. Given the right incentives, people would gladly come forward and become legal. If all they had to do was pass a background check and prove they had a self-supporting job, they would have no reason to fear the process. But they can hardly be expected to identify themselves, their families, and their employers, if there is risk in doing so.

Adding to the frustration of the current system is a flawed application process. Many Americans think these immigrants ought to simply "get in line" and wait their turn for legal entry. The problem is that *there is no line*. Because work visas are applied for by employers, not employees, prospective workers have no way to know what jobs may be available and there is no process for applying. They must either be recruited by a company large enough to afford sending recruiters abroad, or they must sneak across the border and then hope to find employment. Worse, they usually must pay a "coyote" in excess of $5,000 to sneak them across, and submit to the unspeakable abuse that has become far too common. The fundamental issues are the absence of a legal system for a worker in another country to apply for a job in the US, and the absence of a system for employers to find workers if the visa quotas for the year are already filled. Without any solution to those basics, criminalizing either employers or employees cannot solve the problem.

Many employers now post job openings online and potential workers all over the world can see the listings. But the Internet has made the problem worse. The information on the Internet is so voluminous that it is nearly impossible for either a worker or an employer to penetrate all the "noise" to find each other. Even a job posting with very specific requirements generates hundreds (sometimes thousands) of applicants, and employers have no way to sort the real prospects from others. But employment and staffing firms become experts in doing just that, so their services are a vital part of the success of such a program. Their ability to move quickly and accurately in an ever-changing marketplace simply cannot be matched by slow-moving government bureaucracies.

The proposed Red Card Solution would solve the most difficult part of the problem: making noncitizen worker status quick and easy enough that the workers (including those already illegally in the US) will take the steps to get documented. The active involvement of the illegals themselves would make the program work and resolve one of America's most serious security problems. The current system is clearly not working. Unless illegals already in the US believe obtaining legal worker status will be quick and certain, they simply will not apply.

The basis of the Red Card Solution is simple, because it uses the powerful incentives of the free-market system to guarantee the success of a noncitizen worker program. As a result:

- Border control would be easier because workers would go through the gates, not sneak through the fence
- Businesses would have no incentive for hiring illegal workers, because there would be an easy system to find the qualified, legal workers they need
- Workers would have no further incentive to cross illegally, because they would have an easy legal system to find the job they need
- The current programs and paperwork would no longer be needed, because the Red Card would work the same for all

- America would be safer and more secure, because the market for illegal labor would dry up, and everyone but criminals would properly enter through the gates

SEPARATE PATHS

The key to success on this issue is to understand and respect the difference between work permits and citizenship. This has always been the underlying premise of the Red Card Solution. It is vital to keep separate the two different groups of foreigners entering the US, on two different legal paths. One group that wants to become permanent residents or citizens would have to comply with those laws and procedures, established by the federal government, including the vitally important process of assimilating into American culture, learning its history, its government, its language, and the responsibilities required of its citizens. This process was never intended for people simply wanting work; it is for people who want to become Americans.

The second group, noncitizen workers, would follow a different path. It would be a simple way for workers and their families to come to the US for specific jobs, for specific periods of time, and overseen by the private business sector. It would also require them to leave the US at the end of that time, or renew their visas by renewing their existing job, or get another legal job with a new legal visa. Each time the permit is renewed, a new background check would also be required, perhaps every two years. At no time would the work permit provide any special access to the citizenship path.

The distinction between these two paths is both practical and rooted in the Constitution. That founding document makes clear the Congress's responsibility "to establish a uniform rule of naturalization." The federal government has the important task of determining who can come to the US to become an American citizen, and under what conditions. But people also come to the US for other reasons not related to staying long term or becoming American citizens. People visit as tourists, students, athletes, performing artists, businessmen, and as temporary workers. Nothing in the Constitution provides for Congress to determine how many workers are available for a business to hire. Hiring workers is a private business function. The only federal interest in incoming foreign laborers is national defense—the same interest it has in checking incoming tourists, students, athletes, artists, and businessmen—to make sure they are not criminals or terrorists. That's why criminal background checks are important for foreign workers, but once their safety is established, there is no legitimate purpose for government to regulate the number of available workers. But that is also why temporary workers *must* be separate from applicants for permanent residency and citizenship.

Americans clearly understand the difference between the two paths, and they support the specifics of the Red Card proposal. The Vernon K. Krieble Foundation conducted extensive polling on the matter several times over the years, always with similar results. Most recently, a national poll showed a vast majority of people of both parties believe a guest-worker program is the *cornerstone* of any immigration reform:

- Seven out of ten voters favor a guest-worker program for future workers, and for those already in the US illegally
- By a 2-1 majority, voters think the numbers of work permits should be determined by employer demand, not by government quotas
- The private-sector, market-driven, guest-worker program called the "Red Card Solution" is supported by almost 80 percent of the public, including overwhelming majorities among Republicans and Democrats, and among all ethnic groups
- More than 75 percent of people support keeping guest-worker permits and citizenship separate

THE SMART CARD

The use of smart cards for identification and access has become commonplace throughout the world. Such cards are used in millions of business and government buildings, as well as for credit cards and driver's licenses. This plan would create a new noncitizen worker program that is job-specific (no job, no card); is based on work permits (Red Cards) that specifically describe the location, employer, and job for which the card is issued, along with the duration and personal information about the worker, including biometric data. Such information would be encoded on the "smart card" itself in a microchip, making forgery almost impossible.

Such "smart cards" would eliminate the security concerns caused by the current undocumented invisibility. Employers would be able to check the identity and legal status of applicants with a simple swipe of the "smart card," just as they swipe credit cards for payment. The same card could also be swiped and checked by border agents, law enforcement personnel, and others with a need to identify the holder. Legal card holders would be able to come and go across the border, travel to and from jobs, and enjoy all the other protections of the American system. It would remain illegal to hire any worker not in the country legally. More to the point, this would eliminate any incentive employers now have to hire illegal workers, by making legal ones readily available.

If implemented correctly, these smart cards would eliminate the security concerns caused by the presence of so many undocumented foreigners. Current law already requires temporary workers to have valid passports and current Social Security cards, which have proven too easy to forge. But together with the new requirements for the Red Card, the combination would provide the best possible security for America. With those concerns addressed, there is no need for a bureaucracy or committee to set an artificial quota on the number of cards, because the market would keep a constant check on the flow of workers.

Some leaders have told me they could not imagine "no limit at all" on the number of guest workers. That merely proves how little they truly understand about the marketplace. No business hires workers it doesn't need. The market sets a much more powerful limit than any government regulation. Artificial quotas setting limits on visa categories for particular industries simply get ignored to the extent government underestimates the market demand. But there is no way for workers to ignore that market demand. Either there are jobs available, or there are not, and people have no incentive to sneak across borders for nonexistent jobs. The market will accurately determine the number of workers needed every year—many in some years and fewer in other years. If government needs to know how many there are, it could simply look at the databases and count them. But it can never effectively limit that number; only the free market can do that.

We hear the complaint that these immigrant workers will displace Americans from their jobs or will depress wages. But most studies show that when foreigners come to the United States and fill jobs, they supplement US workers, rather than replace them. They make America more competitive in the global marketplace and increase the US economy with their labor and their purchases of goods and services produced here. It's a win-win for American workers and businesses.

If the system for obtaining such cards were simplified, as in the Red Card Solution, all foreigners would be able to have some form of legal documentation: student or tourist visas, permanent resident (green) cards, asylum documentation, or work permits. The latter could replace all the existing temporary work visa categories, but would be completely separate from the current system for obtaining green cards, permanent status, refugee/asylum status, or the process for citizenship.

Workers would have another strong incentive to obtain the legal status if their families could be kept intact. Most other countries issue special permits for families accompanying guest workers, which make them legal, too, but without any special benefits. Under such rules, an estimated four million Americans work and live abroad as "guest workers" in nearly every country of the world. They can and do bring their families, but they are never offered citizenship, nor are they eligible for welfare or other public benefits, nor are their children educated at public expense.

GUEST-WORKER PROGRAMS WORK

Migration across the southern border has been a political issue and an economic reality for more than a century, especially since the Spanish American War. Between 1901 and 1910 almost 50,000 Mexicans were legally admitted to the US, a number that has grown more or less steadily every decade since, reaching 2-3 million since the 1990s. But for the past 100 years or more, illegal border crossings have often outnumbered legal entries to the US, particularly following periods of stricter regulation of immigration. For instance, when Congress mandated literacy tests for immigrants in 1917 the number of illegal border crossings spiked.

The "Bracero" Program, begun in 1942, admitted farm workers from Mexico to alleviate a wartime labor shortage in the US. It was extended several times, and although there were some abuses by employers, making the program increasingly controversial, it clearly reduced the number of apprehensions of illegals at the border—from nearly one million in the early 1950s to a low of 35,000 during the program's heyday in the late 1950s and early 1960s—a 96 percent decrease. When the program was abolished in 1964, the number of illegal border apprehensions quickly returned to one million per year and has mostly remained at that level ever since. Despite all the Bracero program's well-documented problems, it cannot be denied that a legal system of work permits helps control the border. That is a matter of historical fact that today's leaders must consider.

American public opinion on "illegal immigration" is complex but has had one constant: it has always been directly linked to America's economic situation. Wartime labor shortages have always increased demand for labor, leading to more border crossings. The need for farm labor during World War I was so severe that the INS commission temporarily waved the literacy requirement, and during World War II it led to creation of the Bracero program. Conversely, economic downtimes in the US have often led to public demands for crackdowns because Americans needed the jobs. During the first four years of the Great Depression, 345,000 Mexicans were deported, and during the 1954 recession a massive border roundup called "Operation Wetback" led to the deportation of more than one million people.

Concerns about the treatment of farm workers, combined with pressure from labor unions (which have generally opposed all guest-worker programs), led Congress to kill the Bracero Program in 1964, so the flow of illegals across the border has continued to increase. The Immigration and Naturalization Act of 1965 abolished the old system of national quotas and changed the criteria for immigration to a system based on family reunification and needed job skills. Illegal entries into the US have continued to increase. The Immigration Reform and Control Act of 1986 offered amnesty to illegal aliens who were in the US before 1982, imposed fines on employers who knowingly hired illegals, and established a temporary resident category for agricultural workers. But the border control promised by the 1986 Act never happened, leading to the hostility and distrust many Americans feel toward any reform today.

CONTROLLING THE BORDER

For any guest-worker program to work, of course, the borders of the United States must be controlled absolutely, using the best technology and manpower available, to eliminate illegal border crossings. This is central to the workability of any worker program, but with a practical functioning program like the Red Card Solution, it would also be enormously cheaper because it would eliminate the need for clandestine and dangerous border crossings by otherwise legitimate workers. Workers would now enter through the gate, not sneak over fences or under walls. Modern technology should be fully utilized, including cameras, drones, heat sensors, ground-penetrating radar, and other current systems. Our border patrol agents could then concentrate their resources on apprehending criminals, terrorist networks, drug runners, and "coyotes" who transport illegal immigrants in dangerous and inhumane ways.

INFORMATION IS CRITICAL

The first advantage of this system is information: workers would finally know what jobs are available, and employers could identify qualified workers. Employers would simply post jobs with the private employment agencies specifying location, duration, wages, and other required information. The agencies would then find qualified and interested workers, make the match, run the background checks, and issue the cards. Employers would be required to attempt to hire Americans first, not through the current cumbersome bureaucratic process, but by posting the job for a couple weeks first, for Americans only, before foreign workers are eligible to apply. Under this program, the economic incentive to hire local citizens would be very strong because employment agencies charge fees, from both the workers and the employers. After finding the needed workers, employers would have to pay all taxes, and follow all laws that would otherwise relate to hiring local employees. There would be a defined process for renewing the card, or changing jobs, for workers with no criminal records.

ENFORCEMENT

Once it is easy to hire a legal worker with a Red Card, and easy for foreign workers to get a Red Card, then strong enforcement of current laws would be required for the program to succeed. That includes both the laws against coming to the US illegally, and the laws against employers hiring illegal workers. These laws are already very strong (people crossing the border illegally can be banned for life, and employers hiring illegally can be sent to federal prison). But these laws are enforced inconsistently, if at all, partly because there is a general recognition that there is no simple way for workers to come to the US legally, nor for employers to find legal workers. So, the legal system mostly looks the other way. But laws should be enforced, which is why it must be possible for people to enter the country legally.

Border control is essential to eliminate the availability of illegal "cash" workers. Additionally, sanctions against employers who hire illegals would be needed to ensure that workers whose cards were cancelled would return home because there would be no work. Such sanctions would be fair if the system for legally obtaining needed workers were in place (today there is no such system, so criminalizing employers before they have any legal option is wrong). Finally, workers would be required to stay on the job for which the Red Card was issued, and employers would be required to report any worker who left.

That does not mean the permit could not be portable, an important safeguard against abusive employment. The process for workers to change jobs would be as simple as contacting the issuing firm with the new details and getting a new card. But the existing Red Card could immediately be cancelled (as quickly as cancelling a stolen credit card) for workers who disappear, or who commit crimes, making work somewhere else impossible. Workers already in the US illegally could also apply for and legally obtain the Red Card, after proving they have a self-supporting job and passing the same criminal background check.

No other plan considered by Congress or any of the last four administrations would have solved so much of the problem for workers, for employers, for national safety, and border security, as the Red Card Solution. Every bill that was introduced in Congress in the last decade was so complex and voluminous that there was something for every side to oppose. Worst of all is the status quo, which results in unacceptable humanitarian cruelties, and a national security nightmare at the border.

By contrast, by permitting legal workers to come and go across the border at will, the Red Card Solution provides strong incentives for workers to leave their families at home. They often work at lower-end jobs in the US, but nevertheless earn wages that can significantly improve their lives back home. Many of these people work for several years in the US, capitalizing new businesses in their native countries and eventually returning. But, because their stays in the US might be for many years, and recrossing the border regularly is not an option, they feel compelled to bring families along. That results in some of the most tragic and difficult aspects of the issue: anchor babies and birthright citizenship, phony marriages, chain migration, and family separation.

Under the Red Card Solution, illegal migrants would have powerful incentives to apply for the legal cards, go through the background checks, keep their jobs, and obtain legal status. They would do so by the millions if the other elements of this plan were implemented, because once legal, they would have the same rights as any other worker in the US: minimum wage, decent working conditions, and the protections of the legal system. Not all jobs in the US provide the same benefits, of course. Some employers subsidize health insurance, and some jobs require workers compensation coverage, for example. Under this plan, whatever the requirements are for local workers, the same would be required for visa workers. Thus, there would be no built-in advantage for employers to hire foreign workers since they would cost the same. The only difference for employers would be the availability of an adequate labor supply, which is an almost insurmountable problem in some industries today.

The same powerful incentive to come out of the shadows and become legal would apply equally to undocumented people, whether they snuck across the border or overstayed their visas. This is an important distinction in the current debate. It is estimated that 60 percent of the undocumented population originally came to the US legally, on temporary visas, then stayed after the visa expired. These "overstays," as the government calls them, would have the same solution as border crossers under a simple program like the Red Card. There would be no job without a Red Card, so there would be no point in either overstaying a visa or sneaking across the border. Nobody would hire such workers because of the threat of strict enforcement against employers, if it were easy to obtain legal workers. It wouldn't matter how a worker came to America, they would not get a job without a Red Card, so there would be no incentive to overstay.

For more than ten years, the Red Card Solution has been considered at the top levels of government, in Congress, in the administration, and among the major trade associations and think tanks in Washington. It has been discussed with agency chiefs, committee chairs, White House officials, and congressional leaders including the Speaker of the House and Senate Majority Leader. It is very telling that several of these leaders, on both sides of the aisle, explained why they thought it unlikely that such a simple plan could ever pass, for purely political reasons. However, not a single leader has ever said it was a bad idea or that it wouldn't work. The same has been true during interviews with dozens of reporters, commentators, and columnists. Interviews that have begun on a skeptical note have frequently ended with the reporter expressing keen interest in the idea. It illustrates all too clearly how politics, not practicality, often determines policy.

UNDERSTANDING CONGRESSIONAL PARALYSIS

National policymakers in both parties are seriously split on the overall approach to the immigration issue, even though most insist that something needs to be done. Indeed, vast majorities of American voters have been telling pollsters for years that the current system of unchecked "illegal immigration" is unacceptable. A Tarrance Group survey a few years ago attracted the attention of many politicians with its finding that 83 percent of the public said a controlled system "that would replace an illegal immigration flow with a legal immigration flow" is needed. Pollsters on both sides of the partisan aisle have been testing the issue every year since, with virtually unchanged results.

Still, Congress has been unable to act on major reform plans in at least five separate attempts since then, despite virtually universal agreement on the importance of doing something, and despite several complete changes in the majority party controlling both Congress and the White House. The political dilemma for both parties is simple: their major constituencies are divided among themselves, with competing goals.

THE REPUBLICAN DILEMMA

The Republican Party represents constituent groups whose immigration views are widely divergent. Law-and-order conservatives are a critical component of the Republican base nationwide and insist that the current illegal system threatens national security and violates the rule of law. They cannot tolerate continued lack of control over America's borders and will not engage in a debate on a new policy unless and until it begins with complete border control. President Donald Trump articulated this priority more forcefully than any other national leader, yet he encountered more intense resistance than any other.

The Biden Administration's lack of a border policy is undermining our efforts to implement a sane, legal immigration strategy that the American people will support. At the same time, an enforcement-only strategy is not going to have promising results either. No wall will ever be high enough to keep out foreign workers if there is a strong demand for their services.

The Republican Party's political base also includes millions of fiscal conservatives, who express outrage at the use of tax dollars to subsidize illegal activity. They have driven numerous state and local governments to prohibit public funding of services for illegal aliens, and fueled a national debate on issues from drivers' licenses to public education. Granting in-state tuition subsidies for the children of illegals, for instance, has been a "hot button" political issue in at least a dozen states. These are offensive policies to many millions of Americans who believe correctly that they only reward illegality.

Conversely, business leaders (also a crucial part of the Republican Party's national base) are dependent on a workforce that includes huge numbers of migrant workers. These leaders historically oppose major government intervention in the economy and are generally against further intrusion into labor matters. But, some industries would be devastated by the mass deportation of their workforce. Industries like agriculture, services, and construction have become dependent upon these workers. A system that provides for the orderly, continued availability of such workers has become essential to the debate for these groups. The US Chamber of Commerce, for example, has written often about the importance of immigrants as a source of labor to fill jobs it is difficult to find Americans to do. The Chamber strongly supports a plan to bring illegals into legal compliance to reduce the risk of penalties faced by their employers, even though the companies have no reliable way to ascertain a worker's legal status. Most business groups have opposed mandatory verification, at least partly because these government systems have proven unreliable, prone to "false positives" in which legal and illegal workers with similar names become identified as the same person.

Each side wields enormous influence in Washington, DC, and it is unlikely that a solution can be found without each being satisfied. So, the situation remains stymied.

The polarization of the issue among conservative leaders is astounding. About fifteen years ago a "conservative statement of principles" was published in the *Wall Street Journal* and signed by respected conservative leaders over the years, including Newt Gingrich, Mike Pence, Ed Goeas, the late Jack Kemp, Stephen Moore, Grover Norquist, Rand Paul, the *Wall Street Journal* editorial board, Phil Gramm, and the late Malcolm Wallop. A response published a few days later was signed by Tom Tancredo, Michael Reagan, Bay Buchanan, Phyllis Schlafly, David Keene, Dana Rohrabacher, and Paul Weyrich. The first paper argued the importance of the immigrant workforce to the US economy, and the response argued with equal force the importance of controlling the border. A few months earlier, the Heritage Foundation had published another statement of principles by Ed Meese and Matthew Spalding calling for both better enforcement and a simpler path to legal immigration. Even the Heritage Foundation itself has published conflicting "White Papers" on this issue.

Until these varied interests (which are usually on the same side of winning issues for the Republican Party) can be brought together, it is not likely that Republicans can back any new reform plan, however strong public support may be. In fact, it is unlikely even Republicans in Congress will be able to join forces so long as groups like the Chamber of Commerce, Americans for Tax Reform, and Club for Growth have a different perspective than the Heritage Foundation, Eagle Forum, American Conservative Union and so many other icons of conservative thought in America. During the eight years of the Bush administration, Republicans in Congress were never able to bring these conflicting interests together to address the issue. Nor was President Trump able to achieve a solid consensus among Republican office holders despite the party's majority in both Houses for his first two years.

Among Republicans, a solution must be found that gives each side what it needs and promotes America's economic self-interest. One side insists on absolute control of the borders as a prerequisite to the debate, and another needs a system to guarantee availability of the workforce at a reasonable cost. It is possible to do both. They are not mutually exclusive, but no proposal has emerged that meets the needs of each side. The Red Card Solution would do so.

THE DEMOCRATIC DILEMMA

President Barack Obama had the same problem, despite overwhelming Democratic control of both Houses of Congress during his first two years. Many observers expected the immigration issue to be atop his agenda, as Obama had promised during his campaign. They were to be disappointed. Joe Biden has been even worse on the issue by not enforcing the border and supporting hundreds of billions of dollars of government benefits to noncitizens.

Like the Republicans, the Democratic Party also represents constituent groups whose immigration views are widely divergent. Civil rights groups and minority advocates across the country strongly support an immediate and simple process for illegals in the US to come out of the shadows, register, and become legally documented. They support an easy path to citizenship, not only for illegals already in the US, but for new workers who come in the future, too. They make a strong case about the unintended abuse of illegal workers caused by a system that forces them to live in hiding, work for cash, settle for lower wages, and live in constant fear of both the criminal elements and law enforcement. Some of these groups support relatively open borders, and others would simply raise the numeric quotas for visas and for green cards (permanent resident cards). Their primary objective is full citizenship rights for all people in the United States, regardless of how they came here.

A National Council of La Raza official has said that "empowering undocumented workers through legalization would enable all workers to compete on a level playing field while ensuring that the workforce responds to important demands in the economy." Other groups with similar objectives, including the League of United Latin American Citizens, the American Civil Liberties Union, and the League of Women Voters, are an important part of the party's historic political base. They push for equal treatment for all immigrants, regardless of their legal status, from driver's licenses to subsidized tuition.

On the other hand, Democratic constituencies also include powerful labor unions, many of which have a decidedly different perspective, especially on temporary "guest-worker" programs. Unions generally oppose guest-worker programs, arguing that such workers artificially depress wages and take jobs from their native-born American members. An AFL-CIO publication on the subject a few years ago put it bluntly: "Guest-worker programs are bad public policy and operate to the detriment of workers, in both the public and private sector, and of working families in the US." Thus, while civil rights groups argue for an easy path to citizenship for illegal workers and open borders for the future flow of labor, unions have simultaneously argued against any more guest workers of any kind.

In other words, the Democratic Party remains as divided on this issue as the Republican Party. That is why with control of the White House for eight years, and filibuster-proof majorities in both Houses of Congress the first two years and the Senate for four more, Democrats failed to enact immigration reform.

There is also a strong suspicion that Democrats don't really *want* to solve the immigration issue in a humane and economically productive way. Democrats have done well in recent years with Hispanic and Asian voters by simply denouncing Republicans as racist and anti-immigrant. Solving the crisis at the border and having an orderly but expanded visa system would take away one of their favorite political issues. That's not true of all Democrats, but it surely is of many who care about winning elections than creating an immigration system that works. That strategy may no longer be working. Republicans are doing better with Hispanic workers, who want jobs and opportunity, and don't want to be used as political pawns.

During the Trump presidency, Congress was more divided on the issue than ever before. One party was determined to build a wall and secure the border, and the other was equally determined to stop them. Biden has turned a problem into a bubbling crisis.

CAN ALL SIDES WIN?

The Red Card Solution can resolve this dilemma for both parties and all the interest groups. Most aspects of a solution that works for everyone seem simple enough: border control, a practical, legal, guest-worker program, protections for American workers, a workable verification system for employers, and a path to some type of legal status for those already illegally in the US.

That last piece remains the most difficult—how to ensure that illegal workers already in the US will go through the process to get documented. They cannot be expected to "report to deport" and they won't leave the US first unless they are certain they can return. That dilemma points to an important part of the problem that is rarely discussed in policy circles but is very real to the workers. The bureaucratic pace and enormous backlogs that plague government agencies have grown worse over the years. For many workers wanting jobs in the United States, the wait is simply too long, the process too cumbersome, and the cost too high. So, the inability of government to respond quickly to such needs simply adds another powerful incentive for people to come illegally, rather than wait for the legal process. It is not uncommon for workers to wait a decade or more for a visa.

Government employees get paid the same whether they issue visas in a timely manner or not, so they will never have the same incentive to make the program work that private companies would have. Private companies have the oldest incentive there is: money. In business, if you don't get the job done the way the customer expects, you don't get paid. But if you do the job better than others, you might get rich. That is the basis of the free enterprise system that has built and sustained the world's largest economy. The profit motive is the strongest motive of all. That is why the private sector component in this plan is the key to a real, workable solution.

INCENTIVES WORK

Consider how laborers act on the incentives and disincentives the current system provides, because both workers and employers act in their own self-interest. Border control has proven very elusive for decades because the standard of living is so much different on opposite sides of the same border.

The US economy offers powerful incentives for migrant laborers: freedom, opportunity, and higher wages than they can hope to earn at home. Employers, too, must respond to incentives. In some industries, the shortage of available workers means they must either hire illegally or close their businesses. In others, the availability of cheaper foreign labor, working for cash and without the need for paperwork, has created a preference for illegal workers that few employers can afford to discuss, but it is nonetheless real. The lack of serious enforcement of immigration laws has reduced the effects of legal disincentives, so given the pros and cons, millions have decided their situation is better operating outside the law than trying to work within legal parameters that are nearly impossible to comply with.

They do not want to break the law, but the current system provides almost inescapable incentives for doing so.

Government cannot simply pass a new law and make these realities go away. Government cannot change human nature, it cannot make people act against their own interests, and it cannot repeal the law of supply and demand. Changing these behaviors requires changing the incentives. That is what a simple, market-based, private-sector implemented program for work permits would do. Legal workers have an incentive to leave their families back home, because their wages buy a more prosperous lifestyle there than in the US. They have incentives to learn English and develop other skills, because they can get better-paying jobs. Employers would have strong incentives to utilize a program under which they could find all the qualified workers they needed. They would also have a strong incentive to first hire local citizens, because no fees would have to be paid to employment firms. Finally, after both sides had an easy way to be right with the law-abiding, consistent enforcement of strong laws would provide the disincentives needed to ensure compliance, border control, and national security.

Incentives are an essential part of addressing this issue. Only by understanding what incentives and disincentives motivate both the employers and the workers can leaders truly understand why a proposal like the Red Card would solve most of the problem, in a way that is consistent with America's founding principles.

THE BIG-GOVERNMENT ALTERNATIVE

Sadly, very few modern politicians can think outside the confines of government solutions for every problem. Immigration reform legislation pushed by both parties over the past decade has had all the same fatal flaws, which is partly why all these attempts have failed. All the efforts have had one thing in common: they all proposed to grow the government in size, scope, and authority.

The last major bill, the Senate measure proposed by the "Gang of Eight" in 2013, never came close to a workable solution, yet many activists continue making the same argument, supporting the same ideas. There are several reasons why such proposals cannot work:

- *Visa caps vs. employer demand*: It is understandable that some people think Congress needs to cap the number of visas, but every attempt to determine exactly how many employees each industry needs will fail. No congressional committee, and no new government bureaucracy, can ever know how many workers will be needed by each business in future years. The only sure measure is market demand. Government caps have never worked and will never work. They simply ensure that illegal immigration will continue.
- *Costs:* There is never a good estimate for the cost of all the new government activity that would be required to nationalize the foreign labor market, which is essentially what such proposals would do. Many politicians have suggested creating a trust fund from fines and fees on previously illegal aliens, but it would never generate enough money for such an ambitious enlargement of the government. Needless to say, assuming everyone who is now in the country illegally would happily pay all the fines and fees is pure fantasy.
- *One path:* Undocumented people already in the US were given only one choice by the Gang of Eight bill and by many of the current proposals, which is the long and cumbersome path to citizenship or nothing. New guest-worker visas are envisioned for future immigrant workers, but congressional leaders continue to insist on a separate program for those already in the US. They fail to understand that the same simple process could easily work for both.
- *Special deals:* All of these proposals are inevitably filled with waivers, discretionary authorities, and special deals for special groups. (Colorado ski instructors and Florida cruise ship employees are frequently mentioned.) Such exceptions and special "accommodations" are an invitation to cronyism and corruption, not permanent solutions.

THE RIGHT IMMIGRATION REFORM

Every time immigration seems like the hottest issue, both sides begin by announcing their main criteria for reform. But the debate should never be about Republican or Democratic principles. It should be about American principles. The right approach to all issues should be based on the founding principles of the United States: equal treatment under the law, limited government, individual freedom, personal responsibility, free markets, and the rule of law.

The immigration debate is always polarized into two approaches: citizenship for everyone living illegally in the United States, which is just plain wrong; or taking no action at all, and that's wrong, too.

Citizenship is the wrong approach because it devalues the very concept. Being an American isn't about your physical presence; it is understanding and pledging allegiance to these principles. You can't be an American if you don't understand what that means. Taking no action at all simply prolongs the agony of a broken system with millions of victims.

There is a third way, and it begins with a look through the lens of these founding American principles. You'll know the right approach (to this or any issue) when you apply these principles to it. They are the bedrock to evaluating any proposed law.

Instead, what the public sees again and again is politics as usual. It is special deals for special groups, coming from on both sides of the aisle. Special deals for agricultural workers, DREAMers, high-tech workers, and the other "chosen" groups. It is wrong for Congress to set artificial quotas on the number of workers any business can have, let alone taking control of the entire labor market, just as in the attempted government takeover of the entire health-care market.

That is not a principled approach, and it will not solve the problem. Only solutions soundly rooted in the founding principles will do that. Americans must remember what those principles are and apply them to important issues. That is the third way; a way to show the world that American principles are *not* outdated, but remain as essential and workable as when they were first written. It's a way to remind Americans about the core values that define them. Americans do not believe in quotas, nor in treating people differently based on their various group identities. People are not Americans just because they all inhabit the same continent. They are Americans because of their belief in principles and ideals. They are a diverse people, as mentioned earlier, but their strength as a nation is in their unity—not a unity of appearance, success, or talent, but a unified belief that ordinary people can govern themselves.

Workers should be treated as guests, not as "entitled" members of the family. Liberals often argue that anything less than full citizenship would create "second-class citizens." But guest workers are not "second-class citizens." They are not citizens at all.

When you have a house guest, do you immediately put them on your health plan, make them a beneficiary of your life insurance, and add them to your will as an heir? They are guests, not family. Guest workers are entitled to work and to be treated well, not to receive full public benefits.

The guest-worker plan that meets these core American principles has been available to congressional leaders for years, and most are aware of its details. That is why important elements of the Red Card Solution are likely to be the cornerstone of whatever Congress does on this issue—if they ever decide to act at all. If they continue to refuse action, though, it will perpetuate one of the great tragedies of our time.

The way to defeat bad ideas is with good ideas, not with no ideas. Leaders on both sides must work together to solve this issue once and for all. Most important, they must do so in a way that is consistent with principles Americans care about, and that will preserve what is exceptional about America. If we can pull this off, America will be a more prosperous, and more humane nation. Our role in the world, as Ronald Reagan put it, is to be a "beacon of freedom," and immigration is a central part of that American heritage.

CHAPTER FIVE

CITIZENSHIP AND ITS RESPONSIBILITIES

Americans need to draw a deep line in the sand when it comes to attempts to cheapen US citizenship. The idea of giving away membership in American society to anyone who happens to be here violates one of the country's first principles: the fact that it has principles.

America as a "nation of immigrants" isn't an old-fashioned and out-of-date anthem, as some supporters of restricting immigration like to say. It is the idea of our nation forever being renewed with fresh blood and fresh talent and a yearning for freedom that sometimes those of us who were born here fail to fully appreciate. Consider that the staunchest opponents of communism and socialism are the people who lived under these oppressive regimes in Cuba, China, Korea, Poland, and Russia. When politicians like Alexandria Ocasio-Cortez and others speak approvingly of socialism, it is out of an ignorance of how dehumanizing and impoverishing these regimes are in real life, as opposed to how it is portrayed in text books.

Anyone, anywhere, can become an American. In fact, it is said that everyone who believes in freedom and democracy is already an American at heart. That's true because America is more an idea than a place; an idea that people can govern themselves. Still, legally becoming an American citizen is a significant accomplishment, the end of a long and demanding process. An immigrant must live in the US for five years, speak English, learn about American history and government, be of good character, and most important, renounce all other allegiances. They must promise loyalty to the United States and its Constitution, including a promise to defend the country if called upon. Citizenship is a very serious responsibility that comes with two prerequisites: it must be offered by a society under predetermined rules, and it must be voluntarily accepted along with the obligations it entails.

Many politicians have forgotten the importance of citizenship, as shown clearly by today's debate on immigration reform. Some argue that illegal aliens need a "path to citizenship" as part of any reform legislation. It is a cynical argument that belittles the importance of citizenship. It assumes that the very act of breaking America's laws (by entering illegally) somehow entitles one to membership. In fact, many illegals now in the US cannot meet the important requirements for citizenship, however badly the economy may need their labor. Nevertheless, some leaders want to bestow not just work permits, but citizenship, precisely because they want these people to vote. But the reasons behind the American concept of citizenship are more important than votes, elections, or even the need for labor.

The word "citizen" is emphasized repeatedly in the US Constitution. Its concept is so important that the authors used the word twenty-two times. That governing document guarantees some rights to all "persons" in the United States, whether they are citizens or not. But the right to vote is explicitly reserved to "citizens" in five different sections. The original framers, and the authors of the more recent amendments, all understood a fundamental truth: democracy only works if people understand the rules, and the politicians live by the ideals upon which it is built. They must know that *e pluribus unum*, the national motto, means democracy's strength comes not from unifying a culturally and ethnically diverse population.

American citizens, and those aspiring to be citizens, must buy into the principles of individual responsibility and a national commitment to everyone's right to life, liberty, and the pursuit of happiness. This is what makes American democracy unique from all others in the world and, even more to the point, it is what makes Americans one people, not a collection of groups and classes. Only people who understand and explicitly agree to those principles should become American citizens.

Today, America has strayed so far from these important ideas that some leaders openly suggest granting citizenship—including full voting privileges—to people merely because they are physically present in the US. New York State recently granted voting rights to 800,000 noncitizens—many some of whom are illegal immigrants. Other localities want to do the same thing. Not only is this policy unconstitutional, but on practical terms, it cheapens and demeans the country, as well as the citizenship of those who worked so hard to obtain it the right way.

America was founded as a great experiment in self-government. To this day, we still struggle in a world full of people who think democracy is doomed to failure. Some argue that immigrants should not be expected to know more about civics than native high-school students. Maybe so, but the answer is to raise the bar for high-school students, not lower it for new immigrants.

Citizenship should never be granted, or accepted, merely because someone is able to sneak across the border, evade law enforcement, and remain hidden long enough. It should be conveyed carefully to people who understand what it means to be an American—this is why we have citizenship tests—and accept it with a hand over the heart, a lump in the throat, and, yes, in many cases, with a tear in the eye.

AMERICA'S BIRTHRIGHT?

President's Trump once proposed to end "birthright citizenship," and the controversy that sparked highlighted a long-simmering dispute about the qualifications for American citizenship, and the responsibilities that go with it. His statement kindled a national debate that is long overdue, about whether everyone born in the US is "automatically" a citizen.

As virtually all experts on both sides explain, the legal answer comes down to how to interpret the Fourteenth Amendment. Commentators who support automatic citizenship at birth often cite what they call "the plain language" of the Amendment, but it does not plainly support their claim.

The Fourteenth Amendment reads:

> All persons born or naturalized in the United States, and subject to the jurisdiction thereof, are citizens of the United States and of the State wherein they reside.

In other words, there are two aspects to American citizenship: birth, or naturalization in the US, *and* being subject to its jurisdiction. The "jurisdiction clause" has meaning—or there would have been no reason to include it. The primary purpose of the Fourteenth Amendment was to provide full citizenship to recently freed slaves. But the "jurisdiction clause" was included precisely because *not all* people born in the US are subject to its jurisdiction. Many may also have loyalties elsewhere and have not voluntarily pledged allegiance to this form of government.

Michigan Senator Jacob Howard, author of the Fourteenth Amendment's citizenship clause, made clear that the provision did not convey citizenship to "persons born in the United States who are foreigners, aliens, or who belong to the families of ambassadors or foreign ministers." Judiciary Committee Chairman Lyman Trumbull agreed that it meant "not owing allegiance to anybody else and being subject to the complete jurisdiction of the United States."

It is clear from the recorded debates at the time, Congress did not intend to convey automatic citizenship to the children of foreign nationals ("foreigners or aliens"). It made no distinctions about whether they came to the US as workers, tourists, students, or in any other category; their children were not automatically citizens. In today's context, it should make no difference whether they came to the US legally or not. Those details all miss the point of the jurisdiction clause.

The point of that clause was explained by Professor Edward Erler, author of *The Founders on Citizenship and Immigration*. It is the key concept of what the Declaration of Independence calls "the consent of the governed." Citizenship must be offered by the society, and it must be voluntarily accepted by one who understands the duties it includes. His analysis of the Fourteenth Amendment is not just clear legal scholarship; it is plain common sense.

This is the heart of America's founding principles. Americans are all equal under the law, not classified because of where they are born. They are "citizens" whose government only gets "just powers from the consent of the governed." Thus, *new citizens* must "consent" to be governed by this system. That's why the law requires that they voluntarily pledge loyalty to the government, and understand America's history, language, and institutions. The fact that they happen to be physically present does not prove they have "consented" to anything. Thus, treating the children of foreigners as automatic citizens creates a class of "Americans" who have never agreed to those terms.

Notably, Congress has exercised its authority to decide who is "subject to the jurisdiction" of the United States several times before, as with the Native Americans, to whom the Fourteenth Amendment did not initially apply. That was because in 1868 (when the Amendment was ratified), they remained loyal to the tribal nations, not the United States. It took three separate Acts of Congress between 1924 and 1940 to grant full citizenship to the Native Americans, who had to accept it with a pledge of loyalty to the US government, just as new citizens today must pledge.

A Supreme Court decision from 1898 is often cited as proof that the Fourteenth Amendment made no exceptions, but it did not address the meaning of the "jurisdiction clause," nor was the plaintiff in that case born to people who were in the US illegally. Indeed, it was written for a different era, and did not anticipate many aspects of today's immigration issues. It was written by the same court that had just upheld racial segregation, and its conclusions are ripe for a more modern analysis.

A serious discussion of the issue is needed, as well as a new understanding of the importance of citizenship. That may require a new Supreme Court decision, but it does not require a constitutional amendment.

This issue is not about race or national origin. While the children of foreign nationals should not be automatic "birthright" citizens, they most certainly *do* have the right to become citizens. Like anyone else in the world, they may apply, go through the prescribed process, and become citizens. But they must do so when they are old enough to responsibly pledge allegiance to the American form of government and understand what makes it unique and revered around the world.

AMERICAN EXCEPTIONALISM

American exceptionalism is often discussed, and sometimes even used as a campaign issue, but the concept is poorly understood. Some suggest it implies that Americans think they are better than others, or that they are exceptional because they are rich, or free, or have the opportunity for success (things many Americans believe are slipping away). But that is not it.

America is exceptional because its founders set up a framework for a government unique in the history of the world. This government is based on the concept that free citizens can be responsible for themselves, and therefore government should be empowered to do only those things that citizens cannot do, such as provide for the national defense. Individual citizens hold the sovereign power and the government is accountable to them. Each is responsible to protect his own freedom. That is a major factor in what makes America "exceptional."

But therein lies the danger.

Alexis de Tocqueville, the nineteenth-century observer of the American experiment in self-government, wrote in 1835:

> The species of oppression by which democratic nations are menaced is unlike anything that ever before existed. [...] The supreme power extends its arm over the whole community. It covers the surface of society with a network of small, complicated rules, minute and uniform, through which the most original minds and most energetic characters cannot penetrate to rise above the crowd. It compresses, enervates, extinguishes, and stupefies a people [...] reduced to be nothing better than a flock of timid and industrious animals of which the government is the shepherd.

The United States may not have come to that point yet, but it is on the cusp. What could threaten the concept of American exceptionalism would be a government that provides cradle-to-grave entitlements and dependency of people who do not pay taxes, upon those who do. That is a policy paradigm that does not foster exceptionalism, but bondage to the state.

WHY CITIZENS MATTER

Thomas Jefferson wrote, "Every government degenerates when trusted to the rulers of the people alone. The people themselves, therefore, are its only safe depositories." When America's forefathers created the framework for government, it was unique in human history. It is this framework which makes America exceptional. Their words are more powerful than any paraphrase.

> We hold these truths to be self-evident, that all men are created equal, that they are endowed by their creator with certain unalienable rights, that among these are life, liberty, and the pursuit of happiness, that to secure these rights governments are instituted among men, deriving their just powers from the consent of the governed.

In other words, citizens are the sovereign power in the United States, and the government is accountable to them, not the other way around. The American form of government, designed to protect their rights, has been allowed to become an ever-more powerful and despotic entity. Instead of holding the government accountable for its trespasses, most citizens no longer understand the founding documents because the education system has failed them. They have no idea what their responsibilities are as citizens. Of those that do, too many shrug their shoulders and think, "I am only one person; what can I do?"

America's exceptional form of government is an endangered species. If the people do not stand up for the founding principles and reassert the duty of citizenship, it could become extinct. It doesn't have to be that way. Dedicated citizens saved the national symbol, the bald eagle, from extinction, and dedicated citizens can save the American experiment, too. They should think of it as part of their "job description." Again, this is one of the primary reasons why we have public education. To teach people about our history and the privileges and responsibilities of being a citizen of this nation.

Americans who think one person can't make a difference against the power of government should remember that the Declaration of Independence was created by a small group of people working against the world's greatest superpower. As Margaret Mead famously said, "Never doubt that a small group of thoughtful, committed citizens can change the world; indeed, it's the only thing that ever has."

ARE WE READY?

This generation lives at a unique time in American history. When Donald Trump was inaugurated as president, he said in his inaugural address, "We are transferring power from Washington, DC, and giving it back to you, the American people." Then House Speaker Paul Ryan said, "We want to reset the balance of power, so that people and the Constitution are rightfully restored." House Majority Leader Kevin McCarthy added, "We'll continue to overturn excessive [...] regulations and return power to the people."

The emerging consensus among national leaders that responsible citizens should be in charge of the country seemed almost unique in 2016. The idea leads, however, to the critical question: are Americans ready and willing to rise to that challenge?

The American founders laid out the founding principles in the Declaration of Independence. Those principles are still the foundation of the country—that all people have certain unalienable rights, that to secure these rights men have instituted governments, which derive their just powers from the consent of the governed. In other words, the sole responsibility of government is to protect the rights of its citizens, and citizens must give their consent to its actions for them to be legitimate. It has been by inaction, instead, that citizens have consented to the erosion of their freedom.

The call to give power back to the people during the Trump years gave Americans a strong purpose and a reason to act. One election cannot change that. Many people still find a distant federal government difficult to influence, but everyone can be a guardian for liberty in their local communities by attending town meetings, scrutinizing budgets to be sure tax dollars are spent correctly, looking at regulations and proposals to see if they impede freedom, and letting their neighbors and friends know what they find. Working together in towns, counties, and states, an "army" of engaged citizens can restore their freedoms and the ability to pursue their own happiness.

Freedom is continually eroded in seemingly ordinary ways, when we regard government as a security blanket. Tyranny can come from Washington, DC, or the assaults on freedom can come from local governments. For example, citizens of Old Lyme, CT, recently received a letter from the town requiring them to make an appointment for the assessor to make a routine inspection of their home, to ensure their property tax was properly assessed. One owner called the town hall and reminded them of the Bill of Rights and its protection against searches of "persons, houses, papers, and effects" without a search warrant from a judge, issued only with probable cause to suspect a crime. Pushback from one citizen was all it took for the town to back down from an egregious affront to liberty.

Informed citizens are taking similar action on behalf of freedom every day, but more such guardians are needed all across America. The Vernon K. Krieble Foundation's citizenship project, the "Lens of Liberty," was designed to remind Americans of the core meaning of citizenship, its responsibilities, and how to engage with their government. It explains how to look at every issue, proposal, or debate "through the Lens of Liberty." Citizens should always ask whether a new idea, at any level of government, expands or curtails their freedom, and whether it results in more opportunity or less. The Foundation distributed thousands of "freedom kits" with several important tools to show responsible citizens how to do that.

It is heartening to hear national leaders recognize the importance of restoring the Constitutional framework, designed to ensure sovereign power remains with the people, not the government. Senators like Marco Rubio, Mike Lee, Ted Cruz, Marsha Blackburn, and others campaigned successfully by vowing to return power to the people. But voting and electing new leaders is only the first step, and it is not enough. They can only give power to citizens who are ready to accept it, and exercise it responsibly to protect freedom.

Former Speaker Newt Gingrich explained it thus: "We loan power to the state, government does not loan it to the people." But we cannot simply loan that power to the government, and then look away. Keeping a close watch on those we have elected is the central duty of citizenship.

In 1821, Thomas Jefferson warned that "When all government, domestic and foreign, in little as in great things, shall be drawn to Washington as the center of all power, it will [...] become as venal and oppressive as the government from which we separated."

That is why "We the People" must act, and not rely on elected officials to fix everything. Responsible citizenship is the essential ingredient of freedom, because freedom does not start in the White House; it starts in your house.

~~~~

CHAPTER SIX

A NEW RENAISSANCE
OF FREEDOM

When Calvin Coolidge explained the importance of the American flag, he concluded that its primary significance is about the duty of American citizens.

> We identify the flag with almost everything we hold dear on earth: peace, security, liberty, our family, our friends, our home. […] But when we look at our flag and behold it emblazoned with all our rights, we must remember that it is equally a symbol of our duties. Every glory that we associate with it is the result of duty done.

That is, in fact, the principal strength of America today, even in the most trying of times. There are still millions of ordinary and extraordinary Americans performing the duty of good citizens every day, in communities from sea to shining sea. They stand up for their freedoms when they are under assault. These active and engaged representatives of "We the People" are helping hold government accountable for overreach and tyranny in their communities. They inspire many others to take up the challenge of preserving freedom.

UNSUNG HEROES

These people are America's unsung heroes, which is why the Vernon K. Krieble Foundation spent several years publicizing and honoring their work. In partnership with the State Policy Network, Turning Point USA, and several state organizations, the foundation gave major awards to unsung heroes from across America, published op-ed pieces about them, invited them to speak at conferences, and featured them on websites. All Americans should honor the work of dedicated and responsible citizens who work to preserve freedom. Their stories are compelling examples of what can be achieved by citizens who take time to get involved.

- Kirk Allen and John Kraft are known throughout Illinois as the "Edgar County Watchdogs," and their extraordinary achievements in holding government accountable have made them inspiring national models. Neither one of them is a lawyer; neither is wealthy; neither has a law enforcement background. Yet they took it upon themselves to ferret out corruption, and they stand as watchdogs for freedom in Illinois and everywhere. They monitor the activities of their local governments, and they train other watchdogs in other communities, helping spawn a wave of citizen involvement that is truly changing their state. They have endured criticism that would have discouraged many of us, but their work has resulted in more than 100 corrupt public officials being forced from office. They are heroes in every sense of the word.
- Elaine Vechorick is a freedom fighter in Mississippi, whose work has inspired dozens of others. She explains her involvement this way: "I am a business owner, but I can devote about half my time each day fighting for liberty. The happiest day of my life was when I decided to tune out all the national issues I can't influence, and concentrate on state issues and solutions." By focusing on winnable, manageable

battles, Elaine has made a tremendous difference. She led the charge to expand gun rights in Mississippi and launched the successful campaign to eliminate a state auto inspection requirement where fees were levied but no inspections were being performed. She raised grassroots support for bills to reduce Medicaid fraud, to eliminate civil asset forfeiture, and to increase campaign finance transparency. Perhaps most importantly, she has shared her expertise and contacts generously with others of both parties to help them be as effective as possible, too. She used a truly insightful line in her award acceptance speech, explaining that "The biggest enemy I battle is people thinking they can't make a difference." Her work certainly proves otherwise.

- Steve Schopp is an Oregon contractor and a volunteer activist, who has become highly effective in creating coalitions to kill big-government projects. In his Oregon hometown, he helped prevent a $120 million boondoggle that would have diverted funds from essential local services. He built a powerful coalition of allies and used his persuasive ability to kill a massive increase in government spending at the local level. He went on to build a network of like-minded citizens and organizations, to identify fiscally conservative allies. They spearheaded an initiative to require a newly approved county vehicle registration fee to be submitted to a public vote, and despite being outspent by more to 30-to-1, Steve and his allies defeated the measure on the ballot. He teaches fellow citizens that a growing government requires steady streams of tax revenue. By cutting off the supply of cash through grassroots organizing, he has simply killed several local power-grabs, and continues his work unrelentingly. He does not draw a paycheck for his activism, but he is more effective than lots of people who do. He is a force to be reckoned with in the Portland area, with a continuous goal of shrinking government.
- Patti Morrow is an interior designer. When the American Society of Interior Designers (ASID) attempted to take over

that industry through a licensing program requiring a four-year degree in interior design, Patti decided to resist. She created the Interior Design Protection Council to challenge ASID's multi-million dollar lobbying effort. She assembled networks of independently minded interior decorators in each state where ASID-backed legislation had been filed or threatened, and transformed those designers into an effective opposition force, taking on ASID in the media, at state capitols, and in the blogosphere. This sometimes came at great personal cost as Patti quickly became a target of vicious personal attacks from association members frustrated by the effectiveness of her advocacy. Several states were poised to adopt the licensing laws, walling off the trade to all but a small handful of people. It is likely that of thousands of people practicing interior design in America today may still be in business because of someone they have never even heard of: Patti Morrow. She didn't lead this battle for fame and fortune; she just knew it was the right thing to do, and no one else was stepping up.

- Jason Moore owns a masonry business in Odessa, TX. He became concerned about the lack of free-market, pro-capitalism material in public-school textbooks, and testified before the state board of education. He then took on a committee of the state legislature about wasteful spending on what he called "Taj Mahal-type facilities," and showed them how cost savings could be achieved. He became such an effective advocate for limited government that he was given his own radio talk show, where his volunteer work gives voice to taxpayer advocates. He has become known as "Captain Watchdog" and involved his wife "Colonel Watchdog" and their five kids, "the watchdog pups." He uses a website for "barking on behalf of the taxpayer," calling himself a watchdog, not an attack dog, and not a lap dog. Jason is jovial and good natured, though serious about his duties as a citizen. He even put cameras on buildings to see when public officials are at work and holds them accountable.

- Like thousands of mothers across America, Jennifer Parish operated a small day care center in her home for her own child, and several others, to help make ends meet. But when the state government in Minnesota tried to force all home day care providers to join unions, Jennifer Parish said no. She organized a coalition of day care providers and other allies and put a stop to it. Unions in Minnesota are powerful, wielding enormous influence and awash in lobbying funds. But they were no match for the dedicated work of a citizen with a just cause.

- Duffy Mich runs a software company on Long Island and knows how to use a spreadsheet. He also knows corruption when he sees it. In 2013, he discovered that someone had put $500,000 into a bankrupt venture capital company. That "someone" was part of a federal jobs program that "invested" New York State's money into various economic development agencies. With more digging, he found that this one individual was both the provider and the recipient of the money. His efforts to find out more met with stonewalls and threats. One official told him, "If you know what's good for you, you'll let this drop." But Duffy Mich was determined to uncover the people responsible for violating the public's trust. He wrote letters, made phone calls, became an expert on the applicable laws, and contacted the state controller, the Governor, numerous legislators, the federal Treasury Department, and the press. Despite more than two years of delays, the Treasury Department ultimately made New York State return the taxpayers' money, several officials were fired, and the corrupt program was abolished.

- Students are also stepping up to defend freedom on their campuses. Student leader Joshua Recalde's actions were extraordinary in standing up for a young man at Orange Coast College, who was facing expulsion and other charges for videotaping hate speech by a professor in his class. Joshua risked his own life and expulsion in his stand for the rights of students, and for whistleblower protections. His stand for protecting all political ideologies on campus is now in written board policies at Orange Coast.

- Marcus Fotenos achieved great gains for freedom when he was student body president at the University of Colorado. He spearheaded a resolution for free speech everywhere and pushed through state legislation that now prohibits campus "free speech zones." Marcus says that "positive change is not the result of politicians; rather, it is the result of hard work completed by citizens."
- Jake Chalkey was born with developmental disabilities and was not expected to live past early childhood. But, with the help of his dedicated family, Jake has beaten the odds. He almost lost his fight in 2012, when his mother, Christine, was told the state would no longer fund his medicine, even though he was covered by Medicaid. She faced every parent's nightmare but did not give up. She and Jake fought for a change in policy, and won, but that wasn't the end of their story. It began a multi-year effort for this mother and son, who have worked tirelessly to educate the public and policymakers, becoming a voice for those who cannot fight for themselves.
- Russ Caswell stood up against the full power of the federal government trying to take his property through civil forfeiture without any evidence of wrongdoing on his part. He not only won his case, but also helped set an important legal precedent for other property owners.
- Raleigh Bruner successfully challenged Kentucky's "Certificate of Necessity" law, which prevented him and other entrepreneurs from entering the moving industry without the approval of their competition. His work helped inspire several other states to strike down similar laws, proving the power of a good example.

None of these heroes got involved as paid staffers, just responsible citizens taking action. As the founders intended, individual citizens are the greatest watchdogs for freedom. We should applaud their selfless service to helping keep America exceptional.

THE PRODUCT OF FREE ENTERPRISE

The Vernon K. Krieble Foundation is a small public policy organization, not a gigantic endowment, and it has limited resources. (There are many hundreds, and perhaps thousands, of similar foundations large and small that provide financial support for the causes of preserving America's freedoms.) Yet, with a defined purpose and a handful of dedicated individuals, the VKK has called attention to the important duties of American citizenship and related issues for many years, refocused the debate on several important issues, and persuaded leaders to a new way of thinking about America. It is proof that one person, or a handful of committed citizens, can make a tremendous difference.

The VKK was established in 1984 by the family of Professor Vernon K. Krieble, a scientist, educator, inventor, and entrepreneur. Recognizing that the foundation's assets are the product of a free and democratic society, the founders considered it fitting that those assets be used "to further democratic capitalism and the preserve and promote a society of free, educated, healthy, and creative individuals."

EXAMPLES OF EFFECTIVE ACTIVISM

In recent years, the VKK has become involved in a variety of national issues, from strategic missile defense and illegal immigration to the responsibilities of American citizenship. As mentioned in Chapter Four, the VKK's private-sector initiative to break the difficult political deadlock on illegal immigration, the Red Card Solution, attracted major press attention and helped inform the national debate about solutions during several crucial years. The proposal was embraced by many national and state leaders as a viable, workable solution that is based on a principle as old as America itself: the free market.

In a larger and even more fundamental way, the foundation's "Lens of Liberty" initiative was developed to educate Americans on what it means to be a United States citizen, and on the responsibilities that come with citizenship. It was based on the confidence that a citizenry capable of understanding issues from the perspective of freedom's principles can influence outcomes at virtually every level of American life. These initiatives include several different approaches, all designed to illustrate what engaged citizens can accomplish and why they should do so.

The VKK has also supported dozens of nonprofit charitable and educational 501(c)(3) organizations that demonstrate leadership in furthering those objectives, so that future generations can aspire to and achieve their full potential in a free society. These are just a few of the initiatives the foundation has undertaken in that effort and shows how much can be done by a few dedicated citizens.

First, there were initiatives to educate voters, the general public, and key opinion leaders in communities and neighborhoods across the country about America's underlying principles. All Americans, and especially voters, should understand the Declaration of Independence, the US Constitution, the Bill of Rights, and the essential timeless principles in those founding documents. Several projects have helped advance that goal:

- For several years the VKK produced a series of series of one-minute radio commentaries, aired on more than 800 radio stations and heard by more than eight million people on a regular basis, reminding Americans to look at all issues through the "lens of liberty" and protect their freedom. In addition to a number of commercial networks, these have also aired in partnership with Radio America on many of their stations, during popular talk radio shows.
- The "Unsung Hero Award," mentioned earlier, was given at the annual meeting of the State Policy Network for seven years, recognizing everyday people who have fought for freedom in their communities. It included a $25,000 award

and attracted significant publicity to their efforts in defending liberty against government overreach. The VKK also gave similar student hero awards at Turning Point USA meetings, including a $10,000 award for college students who stood up for liberty and pushed back against administrations and faculties that tried to limit free speech.

- Production of a video documentary to promote a broad, general-public understanding of citizenship. It is a free download from VKK websites and has been used at numerous community and neighborhood meetings.
- An interactive Lens of Liberty website provides access to the VKK videos, documents, citizenship tools, and other information, as well as links to other organizations working on citizenship and founding principles issues.
- Frequent use of social media, as well as traditional op-ed pieces, press releases, and newspaper articles about the foundation's work have helped draw attention to issues involving citizenship, and to the available resources the VKK and many others have provided.

Second, several projects were designed to educate immigrants on the same issues, because all new Americans should understand their nation's history, culture, language, civics, and especially its founding principles. In pursuit of that goal, VKK developed a new "American Citizenship Owner's Manual," designed to mimic an automobile owner's manual, in an easy-to-understand format that explains the American ideal, and the unique system based on self-government and personal responsibility. Like a car manual, it begins with a simple description of all the "parts" that make up American citizenship, and includes sections on the privileges of ownership, required maintenance, respecting other drivers, operating the controls, safety restraints, applying the brakes, and handling emergencies. Thousands of these manuals were distributed at CPAC and other gatherings and proved popular especially with young voters.

Third, there were projects to educate American public-school graduates. All students graduating from America's public schools, as new voters, should understand the nation's history, civics, and founding principles at least as well as new immigrants do.

- The American citizenship test has been "dumbed down" to such an extent that new immigrants now must merely memorize names and dates in history, but not the values behind historical events. Nevertheless, the VKK began advocating a system for giving that same test to graduates of public schools, which would call attention to the test's shortcomings, while increasing knowledge of American history. In 2015, Arizona and North Dakota enacted a law requiring graduating seniors to pass the American citizenship test. By the end of 2018, sixteen states had legislated similar requirements. That provides a great opportunity to educate a new generation on the vital principles of American citizenship. The threats to American freedom have been heightened by the pandemic and the government's reaction to it, making civics tests more important than ever.
- The VKK produced modern-language translations of America's founding documents and published a pocket-sized book containing the Declaration of Independence, the Constitution, and the Bill or Rights. Its purpose was simple: language changes over time, but principles do not. These little books are especially popular among home-schoolers and others with the opportunity to discuss the founding documents with young students, in language they can understand. For example, the famous lines in the Declaration that begin, "We hold these truths to be self-evident," are translated into language young students can more easily relate to:

Some facts are so obvious anybody should understand them: All people are created equal; they are born with certain rights that can never be taken from them. These rights include life, liberty, and the pursuit of happiness. Protecting these rights is the reason people create governments. That means governments only have power with the people's permission. Whenever any form of government begins to destroy these rights instead of protecting them, the people have the right to change or abolish it, and to create a new government, setting it up in a way they believe will improve their safety and happiness.

- For several years the VKK also discussed with various educational leaders the community service requirements imposed by many school districts. There should be a much wider range of citizenship and civics projects for students to use in fulfilling those requirements, and for clubs and organizations. In too many schools, the preferred choices tend toward volunteering in community centers, soup kitchens, homeless shelters, and hospitals—all worthy choices, but focused on liberal ideologies. For students learning about serving their communities, it would be just as valuable for them to work in businesses that provide public services, or think tanks or nonprofits on both sides of the political spectrum.
- The VKK worked closely with the Bill of Rights Institute to develop new curriculum materials focused on the responsibilities of American citizenship. That includes new lesson plans such as the "My Impact Challenge," an extracurricular program in which students work in small groups to identify the characteristics of a good citizen and apply that understanding to their roles as participants in their own communities and circles of influence. They study and compare the meanings of citizenship through history, analyze the role of constitutional principles and virtues in a civil society, and engage in civil discourse, demonstrating reasoned judgment while considering varied opinions.

There were initiatives to educate association leaders and members, as well as think tanks, many of which are enormously influential. Conservative groups and their leaders should make it a priority that all their work begins from the perspective of the founding principles, and push programs that further educate their constituencies on those ideals.

- The VKK reworked its own websites, materials, and public statements to reflect that priority, while also maintaining a presence for many years at CPAC, State Policy Network, Heritage Resource Bank, FreedomFest, college campuses, and numerous other conferences and meetings. Booths at various conferences were used to distribute these materials and highlight these initiatives, as well as panel discussions and main-stage presentations on citizenship and related issues.
- In addition to dozens of speeches over the years, this work also included hundreds of news media interviews, all with a purpose to discuss founding principles, and the importance of reestablishing an informed citizenry, one prepared to defend freedom for the next generation at all levels of government.

Finally, there were projects to educate legislators, governors, and other state officials with a similar presence at the American Legislative Exchange Council, the National Conference of State Legislators, and similar gatherings. Discussions about these issues were held with hundreds of federal and state legislators and other opinion leaders over a twenty-year period, imploring them to resist the temptation of government overreach. State legislators were often encouraged to assert their own sovereignty over the federal government on a wide range of policies. Many of them found that idea an unusual breath of fresh air in an age of federal supremacy over nearly every state activity.

In pursuing these initiatives, VKK produced and distributed

several thousand "Freedom Kits" for the use of volunteers and activists in a variety of projects and programs. They were distributed at numerous public meetings, and through the mail via Internet orders for several years. The box included a DVD of the citizenship documentary, the Citizenship Owner's Manual, the modern translation of the founding documents, a folder explaining the founding principles as they apply specifically to various modern issues (immigration, tax policy, social security, energy, and the environment), a brochure explaining the VKK's own Lens of Liberty initiative, and a CD containing several of the best of the one-minute radio commentaries. Some of these materials proved popular even beyond the ability of one small foundation to produce and distribute them fast enough, which illustrates the dire need many Americans feel for better talking points and solid information on founding principles, and how to apply those principles to everyday issues.

Today, armed with such information, and secure in the knowledge that they are not alone, there are thousands of freedom fighters at work all across America, working in their own communities to restore the essential concepts of equal treatment, rule of law, limited government, and personal responsibility.

CASE STUDY: BRINGING CONNECTICUT BACK

In many ways, Connecticut is a microcosm of the growth of government, the loss of personal freedoms, and the devastating impact on the American economy, culture, and way of life. But it seems more ironic in Connecticut than most other places, because the state was such a critical player in America's original cause of freedom.

Connecticut was once one of the most prosperous states in the union and a place with great communities, great schools, great colleges, and the birthplace of great, innovative companies. It became the insurance capital of the nation. Now, as taxes have risen, regulations have mounted, dependency on government has grown, and special-interest groups, such as powerful unions, have flexed their political muscle, the state is losing its greatest assets—its people, its businesses, and its self-confidence. This was a state that for 200 years had no income tax, and when Governor Lowell Weicker pushed through this new tax in the early 1990s, extracting money right out of Connecticut workers' paychecks, the state started down a path of astonishing demise.

There are several organizations working hard to bring Connecticut back to its historic greatness as a place of freedom and independence, especially the Yankee Institute, whose work is crucial in highlighting legislative abuses and scaling back overspending, overtaxing, and overregulation. Working with Yankee and others in the state, the VKK hosted several dinner parties and other small gatherings, to invite influential Connecticut leaders to meet and discuss the state's problems and solutions. The goal was to engage leaders with the resources to help this project, encouraging them also to be donors, board members, or project leaders of several new initiatives.

The VKK also developed two different background op-ed pieces about why Connecticut is in such a desperate condition, what needs to be done about it, and the role active citizens can play. Copies circulated widely throughout the state. The foundation continued production of its one-minute radio commentaries and recorded a number of them focused specifically on Connecticut, to raise public awareness of government overreach throughout the state. It also ramped up financial support for organizations already active in Connecticut, including the Yankee Institute, and began to coordinate in-state grant activities with these priorities, as well as projects highlighting Connecticut history, such as the Colt Museum.

Another VKK project sought to reverse the domination by liberals on college campuses, by helping establish a much stronger presence on Connecticut campuses for effective organizations like Turning Point USA, which, with VKK support, worked to establish several new chapters in the state. The foundation has also worked over the years with groups like Students for Liberty, the Churchill Institute, the Intercollegiate Studies Institute, and others whose work helps keep campus activities and policies more balanced.

Perhaps most important, the VKK strongly supported the creation of a new leadership program in Connecticut, to build an army for freedom that will last for generations. The model was the highly successful Leadership Program of the Rockies (LPR), which has spent more than twenty years building a core of active and engaged citizens, including more than 1,700 graduates who are now in positions of influence throughout the Rocky Mountain region, and in virtually every county of Colorado. VKK has been a long-term major supporter of LPR throughout that period of growth.

Also, with support from the VKK, four outstanding influencers in Connecticut were identified and recruited, and with travel assistance from the State Policy Network, traveled to Colorado every month for the entire nine-month LPR program. They emerged as the core team needed to help launch LPR's first satellite project, the Charter Oak Leadership Program.

The VKK considered this leadership program critical to the effort to take back Connecticut, and committed funding for three years to ensure its successful launch. In fact, its first class far exceeded the grandest expectations. The class size goal was thirty-five students for the first year (about half the traditional size of the Colorado LPR classes), but applications flooded in and the first class kicked off with forty-two impressive leaders from across the state. They included the publisher of *National Review*, a former GOP gubernatorial nominee's wife, six business owners, ten local elected officials, five state legislators, several prominent attorneys, political staffers, heads of charitable and nonprofit organizations, two union leaders, and executives from hedge funds, capital firms, and major corporations, as well as the leadership of the Yankee Institute. The class even attracted two members from Massachusetts, perhaps suggesting another site for expansion of freedom's army.

The successful startup of the Charter Oak Leadership Program completely surprised many observers and allies, who questioned whether such a program could work in Connecticut, which is often called the most liberal state in America. Many were unsure whether it would be possible to find the right people in a place that seemed so inhospitable to the freedom movement. In fact, Connecticut turned out to be fertile ground for such a program for exactly that reason. Supporters, donors, and activists came almost out of the woodwork, jumping at the chance to help get a freedom-oriented Connecticut leadership program off the ground. After special recruiting events in Old Lyme, New Haven, Hartford, Greenwich, and Plantsville, some of Connecticut's best and brightest leaders signed up to help recapture what was once the nation's bastion of freedom and independence. Their excitement quickly spilled over into future classes, and the growing alumni corps will change the course of Connecticut history in the next few years. The program has continued to grow and thrive, and is now LPR's training hub for the New England region.

There is much more to be done, but that corps of freedom-minded leaders is already involved in many community-based projects, while also discussing some of the VKK's suggestions for reinvigorating the state's original idea of liberty.

As in many states, a Connecticut transparency project should be created to make agendas, budgets, and other public information available and accessible to the public, so that responsible citizens can scrutinize the work of public officials, with liberty and free enterprise in mind. There are several organizations poised to assist this effort, such as Open the Books, Reclaim New York, the Edgar County Watchdogs in Illinois, and perhaps others. Such a program could help build an army of "guardians of liberty" throughout the state: people willing to attend public meetings, organize other activists, and begin to raise objections that will help call attention to abuses of power, and roll back government overreach. Such an effort could involve partnerships with senior organizations, local senior centers, and others with time and resources to become involved. Others are discussing the development of specific "what to do in your community" pieces for distribution on websites, and in local networks, at regional meetings, Charter Oak gatherings, or other forums, to show citizens specific ways to engage in the battle for freedom.

These are ideas that have formed the basis of most VKK activity for the past few years, because of the dire need to recapture freedom and liberty in Connecticut. As many observers of the Charter Oak Leadership Program have said, "If it can be done in Connecticut, it can be done anywhere."

The VKK is just one foundation, a small number of dedicated people showing that well-focused effort, based on solid founding principles, can in fact make a difference—in Connecticut, in every state, and throughout America.

CHAPTER SEVEN

PASS IT ON

O n October 30, 2008, just before his historic election as President, Barack Obama declared, "We are five days away from fundamentally transforming the United States of America." Twelve years later, in the midst of the 2020 campaign, Democratic presidential nominee Joe Biden echoed that goal, saying that he saw "an incredible opportunity to transform America."

Transform it into what?

Do Americans want this "fundamental transformation?"

Now we see right before us what this transformation entails. Runaway government spending and multi-trillions of dollars of new debt. Federal control over everything from babysitting, to hair braiding, to tree planting. A doubling of the size of the IRS to meddle into nearly every financial transaction that an ordinary American may engage in. A system of racial preferences. A regulatory structure hanging over seemingly every industry and activity. A set of rules in the face of a pandemic that shuts down businesses, locks Americans into their homes, and requires them to receive vaccinations whether they want them or not. The *New York Times* has said that this transformation would offer Americans "cradle-to-grave" protections. But these are concepts that are entirely contrary to the American founding.

For years, American voters have paid little attention to the extreme language of the left, partly because the agenda was poorly defined, and seemed so outrageously dangerous to our fundamental freedoms that the ideas appeared fringe.

But in the years since 2008 the agenda of the left has become increasingly clear to those who have been paying close attention. It is not about preserving and protecting the founding principles of individual freedom, personal responsibility, limited government, and private enterprise. It is about "transforming" America *away from* those principles.

In the summer of 2020, Vicky Osterweil published a book called *In Defense of Looting: A Riotous History of Uncivil Action.* The title is misleading; the book is about violence, riots, looting, and other law-lessness, not history. The publisher's promotional materials describe it as a "fresh argument for rioting and looting as our most powerful tools for dismantling white supremacy." Osterweil says the battle is much bigger than making some necessary changes to correct past injustices. She says we "need a total transformation of our society" to eliminate private property and free enterprise.

The "climate-change agenda" is a massive, multi-trillion-dollar government intrusion into the economy. It would regulate every-thing from what kind of car you can drive, to what kind of lightbulb you can put in your lamp, to what temperature you can set your home or office thermostat. The invasion of personal liberty is all in the name of saving the planet, and young kids at the age of six are learning of climate change before they learn anything about America or its history.

Barack Obama liked to use the term "audacious." His best-selling book was entitled *The Audacity of Hope.* He started a march toward big government when he came into office during the terrible 2008-2009 financial crisis. The government grew. He proposed $1 trillion in "stimulus" spending. It didn't stimulate much of anything as the economy trudged along.

Then Biden came in and upped the ante, proposing $6 tril-lion in spending—an amount greater than what this country has spent fighting every war to date, building the interstate highway system and intercontinental railroads, and putting a man on the moon. The left preached that the reason the Obama stimulus didn't work was that government didn't spend enough. There is always an excuse in Washington for why government programs fail, why we need to spend more, and why the free-enterprise system needs help.

The fatuous argument against the free market is not new, of course. It is the same argument advanced by Karl Marx 150 years ago, which was the foundation of a communist system that brought the world to the brink of nuclear destruction, and resulted in nearly 100 million deaths through executions, famine, war, forced migration, and slave labor. The "collectivist" argument is not new. What's new is that Americans no longer remember the horrors of communism, because they have stopped caring about and studying their own history. They have lost their memory. Thus, they are vulnerable to any argument that sounds fresh and new, even one as poorly researched as Osterweil's.

Until very recently such a book, written by an activist protester barely out of college, would have received little attention. But in August of 2020, *In Defense of Looting* quickly became Amazon's number one new release, and the author is being touted as one of the country's most important new voices, in the same way a doting press took a twenty-nine-year-old freshman congresswoman named Alexandria Ocasio-Cortez, who had never held a job before campaigning for public office, and made her a national star.

"This society we live in under capitalism is entirely structured around the production [and] circulation of commodities," Osterweil writes. "It is a cruel system, built for the creation and revocation of things, not for the flourishing of people." The solution, according to this twisted logic, is for poor people simply to take what they want. "Looting represents a material way that riots and protests help the community," she writes, "by providing a way for people to solve some of the immediate problems of poverty."

The open invitation to theft, of course, ignores the "rights" of the victims, focusing instead on the real purpose of such lawlessness. "The right to property," according to Osterweil, "is innately, structurally white supremacist." This implies there is no way under the American system for people of color to own property, which is demonstrably wrong. It is a view that can only be held by people who do not understand America's history, economy, culture, and way of life. Nor would such a view be of concern, except for the millions of Americans who apparently share it—people who have forgotten who they are, and what their country is, if they ever knew.

The misunderstanding and mischaracterization of capitalism underscores the entire argument of the left. Osterweil, and other poorly educated activists, lament that the "society we live in under capitalism is entirely structured [to the disadvantage of some groups]" and was "built for the creation and revocation of things." But it isn't "structured" at all, nor was it "built" by anyone, for any purpose. What they call the "capitalist system" isn't a "system" at all. It is merely the freedom to buy and sell goods and services in an open marketplace, something Adam Smith called "the invisible hand." It evolved in the absence of government control, not because of any government decision. Socialism, by contrast, is properly defined as a "system," because it operates with a defined set of rules and procedures. Under a socialist system, government owns the property and means of production, decides what jobs fit particular individuals, and determines how and where people can live their lives. It is the alternative to—the opposite of —freedom. Americans who have forgotten that distinction are vulnerable to influence from activists who twist the truth to push the agenda of socialism.

THE GOOD NEWS

It is easy to become worried when Americans seem so divided on the fundamental differences between freedom and totalitarianism, and when socialist candidates win millions of votes and sometimes get elected in the freest country on Earth. But there is another side of that coin. Whether Americans remember their history or not, whether they understand the founding principles or not, they do understand the prosperity that separates them from much of the world. They have just forgotten why.

Some Americans apparently feel guilty about that prosperity, which is almost understandable when they are constantly bombarded with messages about America's failures and mistakes. We are told by the left and the self-proclaimed "social justice warriors," that income inequality and "racial injustice" can only be solved by government. But for all our problems, and in so many ways, America has the most opportunities for minorities, for disabled people, for the poorest among us. Minority advancement has been a hallmark of American greatness, especially in the last half century. A strong case could be made that the advancement of black Americans has been slowed by government programs. This was the title of a famous book called *The State Against Blacks* by the late black economist Walter Williams. He showed that it was actually government programs like the minimum wage and welfare payments that increased black unemployment and helped break up the traditional family structure in black communities.

Very few of these social justice warriors who find fault in so much of America make the choice of moving to other countries, though all are free to do so. On the contrary, millions of immigrants from all over the world still see America as the place of opportunity and freedom, and while masses strive to come to America, virtually none are clamoring to leave.

The truth is that freeing the human mind has led to the greatest advances in human progress, and created history's freest, most powerful, and prosperous civilization. That happened only because the United States is a country governed not by great rulers, but according to a set of defined principles, laid out in writing, and designed to protect the individual freedom of its citizens. Americans would feel much better about their country, with all its faults, if they at least remembered that.

TAMING THE WILDERNESS

In the comfort of the modern world, it is easy to forget how inhospitable the world can be. The old saying was that for most of humanity, "life on earth was nasty, brutish, and short." Nature is often cruel, and for thousands of years people did their best to survive through gathering and hunting, and subsistence farming. Primitive societies were largely unchanged for centuries, with heat, light, and power supplied mostly by animals and human labor. People lived in what is now considered abject poverty, starvation and disease were commonplace, medical science was mostly superstition, and the average lifespan was about thirty-five years. Alex Epstein of the Center for Industrial Progress argues that the use of technology and energy has transformed the natural environment into a livable one. "Most of the natural world is too hot, too cold, has too much rainfall, or not enough," he begins. "Then there's bacteria-filled water, disease-carrying insects, tornadoes, earthquakes, and tsunamis, to name just a few of nature's unpleasant features." Yet, despite nature's inhospitable side, most Americans now live in a world that is astonishingly comfortable, so comfortable that many have forgotten what it was like before.

When the first settlers came to America in the seventeenth century, their lives were simple. They worked from sunup to sundown to eke out a bare living on marginal farms, chopped wood, hauled water, milked cows, and died young. But in America, that was never the end of their story.

In America, the ideal of liberty was more than philosophy; it became official policy, the basis of an entirely different approach to government. In America, people were free to pursue their own happiness, to try new ideas, to succeed or fail based on their own hard work and good ideas, and to prosper by the fruits of their own labor. Today's Americans have forgotten the importance of that freedom, and now want government's protection against failure.

The idea of equality, as Paul Driessen of Heartland Institute wrote, "Emboldened otherwise ordinary people to invest, invent, and take risks. Once accidents of parentage, titles, inherited wealth, or formal education no longer controlled destinies, humanity increasingly benefitted from their innate inspiration, perspiration, and perseverance." The result was that human health, prosperity, and life expectancy increased, "slowly but inexorably at first, then more rapidly and dramatically. Today, the average American lives longer, healthier, and better than even royalty did a mere century ago."

In fact, the richest man in history, John D. Rockefeller (whose fortune adjusted for inflation was five times that of Bill Gates's) lived without air conditioning, feared now-obsolete diseases, and traveled slowly and uncomfortably on dirt roads and dusty trains. He had many servants to prepare his food but could not get fresh fruit or vegetables out of season, and never tasted a burrito, a pizza, Szechuan pork, or Chilean sea bass. Even his exalted lifestyle was in stark contrast to today's Americans, with supermarkets where ordinary people can get fresh food year-round, at reasonable prices, from all over the world. The wealthiest kings of the Middle Ages could not have imagined today's interstate highways, international airports, central heating, indoor plumbing, regular trash pickup, and antibiotics. Have Americans forgotten so soon what life was once like?

Modern insecticides control the damage from insects that destroy crops and carry diseases. Modern fertilizers increase crop yields beyond what could have been imagined a century ago, when the vast majority of Americans worked on farms. Mechanized equipment has freed people from backbreaking labor, so that today fewer than 3 percent of Americans live on farms, and they feed not only the US, but much of the world. In addition, they use less land and water than ever before, thanks to hybrid seeds, drip irrigation, and other advances. Yet, in the advanced state of amnesia, many Americans no longer remember the stories of their own grandparents.

Millions of Americans share memories of watching grandmother spend hours doing housework, like washing dishes, doing laundry, and hanging it out to dry. They called it "laundry day" because that's how long it took. Labor-saving appliances were among the great advancements of the last century, especially washing machines and dish washers, which freed generations of women from the drudgery of such chores.

American free enterprise freed the human mind and spirit to invest, invent, create, manufacture, and grow. The development of affordable energy made a comfortable lifestyle available not just to the wealthy, or those in large cities, but to everybody. Coal, oil, and natural gas replaced whale oil and other primitive fuels with portable energy that powered trains, farms, factories, automobiles, schools, hospitals, offices, and homes year-round—and saved the whales from extinction. Today, those same fuels also power the technology to remove harmful pollutants from the air and water, and they make possible the manufacture of solar panels, wind turbines, and other renewable-energy equipment.

The growth of economic progress was faster in America than any place on Earth, because of the freedom to create, and to profit from, that creation. By 1925, half of all American homes had electricity, and within fifty years virtually all of them did. RCA began selling radios in 1922 and within a dozen years 60 percent of all American homes had one. In 1950, only 9 percent of American homes had a television, but by 1960 almost 90 percent did. The World Wide Web was created in 1989, and today nearly 90 percent of American homes are connected through desktops, laptops, and smart phones.

That same creative freedom transformed medical science in America, and then around the world. Inventors and researchers discovered bacteria and the causes of diseases that had killed untold millions: polio, malaria, smallpox, cholera, typhoid fever, tuberculosis, and the plague. Vaccinations, antibiotics, x-rays, anesthesia, and better sanitation transformed the lives of generations. By 1900, the average American lived to be forty-six; today they will live to be almost eighty.

From steamboats to railroads, from cars to computers, Americans have always relied on constantly improving technology to improve their lives. Their faith in private-enterprise has never failed to produce advances in the quality of life, in every generation.

NO ACCIDENT

The great advances that allow modern Americans to live such comfortable lives were not an accident of history, or a quirk of nature. They were the direct result of a system based on equality under law, and a right to the pursuit of happiness.

Sadly, the loss of America's memory, and the escalating attacks on its ideals, are also no accident. They are the cleverly designed, carefully orchestrated, and well-funded strategy of people who seek the overthrow of America's founding principles. They are radicals who never really believed that ordinary people could govern themselves, without the control of leaders with superior intellect and breeding. That essential difference of philosophy has defined America's struggles since the Mayflower Compact in 1620.

It has often been said that people who do not study history are destined to repeat it, which is true in terms of repeating past mistakes. But America's national amnesia is actually worse than merely repeating history's errors. This collective memory loss is costing Americans their national identity, which is their character. The traits that defined Americans for two centuries—rugged individualism, bravery, independence, and self-reliance—are rapidly disappearing.

Americans have always tried to care for each other, to provide for those who face special difficulties, and to provide alternatives for those who cannot be self-sufficient. But, perhaps in a rush to empathy and sympathy, they also try to provide comfort to people who simply do not wish to work. Some trace this trend to a school system that began years ago to change the rules of competition, perhaps forgetting that competition itself is the basis of the entire economy. Students are not always encouraged to win, which is now considered unfair to the losers, so all get a participation trophy. If no one teaches students why competition is important, is it any wonder that they become adults with no understanding of free enterprise?

The socialists who have gained such influence in American politics today are taking full advantage of the public's amnesia. They insist on granting citizenship to anyone who makes it across the borders, even terrorists and drug dealers, undermining the citizenship process, and filing the country with millions who are not committed to the founding principles. They foment the kind of chaos, rioting, looting, and unrest that is essential to undermining, and ultimately changing, a government. People who forget their history do not recognize the same tactics that led to the Bolshevik Revolution, the rise of the Nazis, and Mao's takeover of China.

Americans have begun to accept a contrived standard of "political correctness" and "wokism" that changes the language, stifles free speech, and labels not only the people, but the system itself, as racist. They are already forgetting that it was Americans who sacrificed 360,000 lives to end slavery, who strove for another century to eliminate systemic racism, and who effectively did so with the civil rights legislation passed sixty-five years ago.

With rare exception, today's Americans are not racists, nor do they openly tolerate racism. Yet the fear of that label has cowed them into accepting reverse discrimination on a massive scale, and the separation of people into classes and groups to be treated differently, which emasculates the first principle of the Declaration of Independence that all people are created equal. Indeed, it is the racism label itself that has divided Americans into groups, separating them by race and other categories—which is the definition of racist. In other words, the fear of being called "racist" is making Americans become more racist, despite their best instincts, and upending more than a century of their history. It is a modern cultural shift that completely contradicts the lofty dream of Martin Luther King, Jr., that people would "not be judged by the color of their skin, but by the content of their character."

Americans have honored Dr. King for decades, a fallen hero of freedom's march. They celebrate his birthday and have named over 950 streets in forty-one states after him. But, do they remember his words, his work, and the messages of his life? Sadly, Americans have simply lost their memory, forgotten who they are, and even if they do remember, they are too afraid to say so, for fear of being branded racist, sexist, or bigoted against someone. When confronted by Black Lives Matter activists (whose real meaning is that black lives matter *more*), they dare not even think the most obvious response, which is that "all lives matter." To utter those words aloud is tantamount to admitting a vile form of racism. Support for law enforcement is said to be the same as support for racially motivated murder.

In their hearts most people know they are not racist, yet they bow to the power of political correctness, almost in the same way they once feared the accusations of McCarthyism. "Are you now, or have you ever been, a member of the Communist Party?!" Today, people are almost as afraid of the modern version: "Are you now, or have you ever been, a conservative, a Republican, or an advocate of the Constitution?!"

The same socialist agenda that coopted the civil rights agenda also took over the once-genuine agenda of the environmental move-ment. Increasingly radical groups, often funded by foreign inter-ests, have stopped the sound management of public lands. Listings under the Endangered Species Act caused the closure of hundreds of sawmills, the loss of tens of thousands of jobs, and left behind a trail of decimated communities and businesses. Environmental socialists have devastated the ranching, farming, and mining indus-tries, stopped public recreation in hundreds of areas, and closed vast expanses of public land to almost all public uses. At least one result has been more than 100 million acres of forestland burned by catastrophic wildfires that have destroyed tens of thousands of homes and killed hundreds. These fires are a consequence of the lack of management for more than a generation, the failure to properly clear the overgrown forests choked with unnatural quantities of trees, brush, and grasses that the federal managers euphemistically call "fuel loads." Worst of all, Americans almost never question the environmental agenda, because they fear being branded as anti-environmental. It is further evidence that Americans have forgotten who they are (virtually no Americans are anti-environmental) or are afraid to talk about it.

If Congresswoman Alexandria Ocasio-Cortez had proposed the "Green New Deal" in any previous generation, she would have been laughed out of the room. Her proposals have called for a complete end to the use of affordable energy, along with banning beef, eliminating airplanes and automobiles, imposing 70 percent taxes, and subjugating citizens to a one-world government. Yet she is not considered to be an undereducated fool, but a rising star on the political stage, the national spokesperson for the largest faction of the Democratic Party.

Such leaders are pursuing an agenda that should be crystal clear to any observer: to change the American form of government. History, should people decide to study it, is filled with the stories of countries whose governments fell, not to invasion from abroad, but to radical movements from within. America might expect the same future if its people (the only guardians of their liberty) do not recover from this amnesia.

Remember, America is not just a geographic place, but an ideal. People do not have to be born in the US, nor share any certain ethnicity, language, religion, or culture, to become an American. The idea that being an American is defined by principles and values, not by birth, is the noblest definition of citizenship ever established. It is also perhaps the most difficult to live up to, because people are not perfect, as Adam Kirsch wrote in a *Wall Street Journal* article, "American Patriotism is Worth Fighting For."

Kirsch cited Lincoln's second inaugural address, in which he suggested that the divine purpose of the Civil War was that "all the wealth piled by the bondsman's two hundred and fifty years of unrequited toil shall be sunk, and until every drop of blood drawn with the lash shall be paid by another drawn with the sword." Kirsch writes,

> It might seem strange to call this an expression of American patriotism, but in the deepest sense it was. In accepting punishment, Lincoln affirmed that America should be judged by its own highest principles. After all, it is only those principles that make America what he said it was [...] "the last best hope of Earth.

Even Frederick Douglass shared that hope, in his famous July 4 speech where he warned "The blessings in which you this day rejoice, are not shared in common. The rich inheritance of justice, liberty, prosperity, and independence, bequeathed by your fathers, is shared by you, not by me." Yet he concluded with optimism about America's future, because he drew "encouragement from the Declaration of Independence, the great principles it contains, and the genius of American institutions."

"TO FORM A MORE PERFECT UNION"

America is not perfect, and never was. Nor are Americans saints. If we were, we wouldn't need a government or a constitution. We have the sins of slavery in our past, as virtually every nation on earth does. But self-government is an evolving "American experiment." Yearning for "the good old days," or trying to extinguish the sins of our past, is a fool's errand and an exercise in futility. Not only is it impossible to "turn back the clock" and return to yesteryear, but also because no time in the past was faultless and no time in the past provided the safety, security, living standards, and opportunities that exist today. It is, rather, the purpose of every generation of Americans to achieve higher standards, and to get closer to the lofty goals established by the founders, to leave America even better than they found it. Every previous generation has done that.

Will ours?

One generation tamed the wilderness, and established farms and communities across the continent, though at a terrible cost to the native tribes. Another finally ended slavery, though at a cost of hundreds of thousands of lives, more than all the other American wars, from the Revolution through Vietnam, combined. The next generation presided over an industrial revolution that built the great cities, brought technology to the farms, and previously unimaginable prosperity to millions. Other generations of Americans fought two world wars, liberated oppressed people, rebuilt Europe in the aftermath of war, and protected freedom and democracy from worldwide despotism. Others extended democracy's promise of voting rights to women, Native Americans, and other minorities; fought the spread of communism in Asia and elsewhere; ended Jim Crow laws and passed the strongest civil rights protections the world had yet known. Today's activists clamoring to undo America's institutions have completely forgotten those achievements, if they ever learned about them.

We really do, as a people, stand on the shoulders of giants who bequeathed to us this land of freedom and opportunity.

America's amnesia does not have to be permanent. For individuals, sadly, there is no known cure for dementia. But, for a nation, there is. Individuals suffering from Alzheimer's cannot decide to study their history, ask others to share their memories, read books and articles about the past, and suddenly regain their memory. But nations can. There is an antidote, a vaccine, for America's disease and it is not complicated.

If Americans focus on recapturing their history, they will discover that every generation has made great progress toward fulfilling the promises of the Declaration of Independence. They will see American history as a slow and painful, yet steady and relentless, pursuit of freedom. Every generation has also made mistakes: slavery, the trail of tears, Jim Crow, prohibition, and leaving future generations with an unconscionable national debt, among others. This must be taught to children. What kind of nation teaches its children all of its country's flaws but keeps them ignorant of its rich history of accomplishments? Patriotism is almost seen as a vice, not a virtue.

What will be the legacy of this generation? Will it let the American experiment die on its watch, because the people forgot what it was all about? Or will Americans regain their memory, reestablish their national character, and continue history's steady march toward a more perfect union?

INDEX

CPSIA information can be obtained
at www.ICGtesting.com
Printed in the USA
JSHW051959151122
33252JS00010B/344